THE ULTIMATE GUIDE TO BLACK BEAR HUNTING

THE ULTIMATE GUIDE TO BLACK BEAR HUNTING

Douglas Boze

Skyhorse Publishing

Skyhorse Publishing books may be purchased in bulk at special discounts for sales promotion, corporate gifts, fund-raising, or educational purposes. Special editions can also be created to specifications. For details, contact the Special Sales Department, Skyhorse Publishing, 307 West 36th Street, 11th Floor, New York, NY 10018 or info@skyhorsepublishing.com.

Skyhorse® and Skyhorse Publishing® are registered trademarks of Skyhorse Publishing, Inc.®, a Delaware corporation.

Visit our website at www.skyhorsepublishing.com.

10 9 8 7 6 5

Library of Congress Cataloging-in-Publication Data is available on file.

Jacket design by Tom Lau
Cover photograph by Justin Haug

Print ISBN: 978-1-5107-0979-9
Ebook ISBN: 978-1-5107-0980-5

Printed in China

Contents

———

Dedicated to my wife Amy and to my boy Haydin.

Introduction

They walk mainly unseen through the woodlands and brush, maybe even through your neighborhood. Skirting prickly-pear patches and digging under acorn trees, cruising along cornfields and down creek bottoms, the herculean dark figures own the territories they travel. Small brown eyes, an always searching nose, keen ears, and enough claws and power behind them to get the job done, black bears are creatures to be admired, respected, and sought after. They are not graceful like deer but have agility similar to their ungulate prey. Loud and unafraid when comfortable, they can slink away just as quietly as a deer wanting to go unnoticed. They are really a contradiction of sorts, an apex predator that viciously attacks fawns and elk calves but enjoys fruits and berries just the same. How can you really characterize black bears? The truth is, I don't think you can. I think they are in a category all their own among big game. Hunting black bears specifically also puts you as a hunter in a category all your own.

I've been hunting big-game animals since I was twelve years old. Some of the happiest times in my life have been hunting with my late grandfather, my siblings, and my dad. It truly saddens me when I meet someone who doesn't like hunting—or, worse yet, hates hunters. It saddens me because they think hunters are bloodthirsty, poaching slobs with little or no regard for nature, in part thanks to Hollywood drivel. Several anti-hunters I have met would like to do away with all hunting. It bothers me for probably the same reason that it might bother you. If they want to do away with hunting, that means they would also deny the upcoming generations some of the happiest times, quite possibly, of their lives. If that were to happen, it would be a great loss to our country and heritage—not to mention, yes, even our wildlife.

Why are my hunting memories happy memories? Was it because I was successful on every single trip out and that hunting was as easy as they show on TV or on an overproduced cable show? Not really, no. I wasn't successful hunting until I was fourteen—and by successful, I mean that I killed an animal. Even then, it was a black-tailed deer spike I shot with my grandfather's 12-gauge shotgun. I was so proud of that spike, I rode in the backseat of the Bronco all the way home looking at it.

The truth is, I spent my first few years hunting with boots that were hand-me-downs, way too big for me, and leaked. I carried a .30-.06 lever-action that I was more gun shy of than accurate with. I stumbled around, fell over logs, and got soaked and cold, all the while rarely seeing deer of any sort. I am sure, due to my clumsiness, anyone walking with me would not see any game either. My Uncle Joe can attest to that—which he told me as I got older. Thank goodness for the patience of loved ones when it comes to introducing hunting.

Yet, I continued to hunt. It was time with my family, friends, and nature that drew me further and further into my passion for the outdoors. I cherished sharing the times in the often miserable weather, dragging ourselves back to my grandpa's Bronco, busting out a Coleman propane stove, cooking up a few cans of Dinty Moore with some butter rolls and hot coffee while overlooking some wooded gulley in the pouring rain. You see, I like to hunt not because I am bloodthirsty. I like to hunt because it gets me closer to nature, closer to my family, closer to the Almighty. I am fulfilling what I am designed to do. People who do not hunt are truly missing out on the human existence, in my opinion.

By nature's design, I am not supposed to go to a drive-through window and eat out of a sack. That is not what humans have done since the dawn of time. What have we done as a species? We have hunted since the dawn of time! I am supposed to earn what I eat—a healthy, low fat, free-range animal that I respect to the highest degree. I am supposed to chase animals, to learn to track and follow, to learn to call to them, to learn their habits, what they eat, where they roam, why they do what they do, how they find food, and so on. Hunting and fishing, by definition, are natural ways to feed oneself and family—as natural as humans could possibly hope to get. Being a hunter is what we are designed for and therefore is what I am at the very core of my being.

So when you meet an antihunter or someone on the fence about hunting, be articulate and explain why you love it, how it feeds your family, how it is the greenest activity a person can do in this modern society. Perhaps you can persuade others to think twice about hunters, who are real people, grandpas and grandkids spending time together, fathers and sons enjoying the outdoors, mothers and daughters carrying on traditions, and husbands and wives building new ones. Explain how license fees and tags are used to help support game and nongame species alike and how without those funds we would not be supporting wildlife efforts against poaching. Thanks to the Pittman-Robertson Act of 1937, hunters and fishers alike have raised more than eight billion dollars, according to the US Fish and Wildlife Service data collected in 2013. Hunters, and their money, are the best friends of an animal.

Now, really, I have to ask you, why are you interested in bear hunting? Is it their super strength? Perhaps it is their cunning? I am sure for some of you the nice, full winter coat of the bear is very appealing. I can tell you why I am so infatuated with bear hunting. There are actually several reasons why. Black bears to me are amazing animals in strength, stealth, and overall beauty. But they can be deadly—and, to me, that is what is so appealing about them. They can stalk you just like you are stalking them. There is a degree of danger in hunting bears that is greater than that of chasing deer, and if you have not hunted bears before, you had better be well aware of the danger.

Black bears can be predatory to humans, however unlikely. Most times you see a black bear, it will bolt to safety, especially if it smells you. It does not want anything to do with you. But if one does attack, it's predatory in nature. It is trying to kill and eat you, so you best fight back as if your life depends on it. Don't play dead like you are supposed to do with grizzlies. A few fatal, predatory black-bear attacks on humans have occurred in the past few years, and the number will likely increase as the black-bear population increases. Numerous states across the lower forty-eight are showing a massive jump in the black-bear population. With increased development and human population growth, it is important to continue to manage the bear populations through regulated hunting.

Several states are being overrun with black-bear populations, including New Jersey. Bears have now been spotted in all twenty-one of New Jersey's counties. People have more and more issues with bears getting into their garbage or roaming in backyards. It's not just the Garden State's problem either; Florida is also experiencing a population growth. As I write this, Floridians are enjoying their first bear hunt since the mid-1990s. In my opinion, black-bear population growth is a great thing. They are wonderful animals, and our world is better with them. Bears do like to get into trouble with people at times. All too often, this is just as much the fault of humans as it is of the bears.

People not securing their trash or leaving out dog food or other edibles for bears to smell and be attracted to spell disaster. But how do you deal with black bears being too close to home? Along with good housekeeping comes sound management by state game departments based on science, not political emotions. A hunting program in states with bear populations that can sustain it is nothing but an economic benefit, bear deterrent that helps enforce the healthy fear of humans, and ensures a wonderful tradition for many families to carry on—not to mention some of the best breakfast sausage and pepperoni sticks known to man.

Issaquah is a town resting on the foothills of Snoqualmie Pass in Washington. It has had a human population boom in the last decade or so, as it is an upper-scale suburb that allows for an easier pace of living within a short drive to Seattle (depending on traffic, of course). However, they have had bear issues every spring and summer as citizens further encroach on the bear population's home range. It isn't the bears' fault, and it really bothers me to hear people complain about bears in their backyards, which is common on local news broadcasts. The bears were there first. It is often some of these city folk who look down upon hunters, as well. The very people who are taking over the bears' home range have the audacity to complain about bear hunters who help manage bear populations and support wildlife, both game and nongame species alike, with the license and tag fees. The antihunting mind-set never ceases to amaze me.

Bear hunting has grown more popular in the last several years, not just in Washington, where I reside, but seemingly all over the nation. Hunters are beginning to realize what fun it is to chase black bears. They are finding out how challenging it can be to find bears and what wonderful and tasty trophies they are. Compared to hunting deer or elk, hunting bear is night-and-day different. Bears are generally solitary animals, which makes them a challenge to locate. You won't see any bear herds when you are walking by a cornfield that has been harvested like you might with deer. You won't hear a bugle from bears during the rut like you would from elk. Yet the allure of bear hunting is drawing in hunters from all walks of life.

The question asked most of me by people who do not hunt bears (but still hunt other animals), specifically, is how to find them. While they are hunting deer or elk, most hunters just stumble upon a bear as it is walking a logging road or eating an old deer carcass. Very few know specifically what to look for when searching for bears. This book will give you all the information you could possibly need to get started in your quest to hunt bears, or it will help sharpen some of the bear-hunting skills you already have. It is true, you can teach an old bear hunter new tricks. After all, I learn a few new lessons almost every time I go out—taught by bears, of course.

Do you live in Michigan or Maine? Have you been hunting bears with bait or dogs before? If so, have you ever tried using a predator call on a bear in the dense northern woods? If not, you really should try it. It is an absolute rush to call bears. Say it can't be done? Say it is just too thick in the woods and it is impossible? I bet it can be done and have proven it so, personally, in the dense underbrush of Washington (literally solid walls of blackberries) and Idaho (steep, rugged, leg-burning terrain) to the choked willow and alder thickets of Alaska. Now, am I knocking those who hunt bear with bait or dogs? Never! I am offering new bear hunters and old-timers new ways to approach bear hunting. Never baited bears before but finally have the chance to do so? This book will help you out with that, too. From where to set up bait sites to how to initially draw bears into your site and more—I've got you covered.

It is my hope and goal that you find this book unlike your typical hunting book. I have composed what I believe to be the most comprehensive information on the subject. It is filled with the dos and don'ts of bear hunting while not overloading you with tons of banter about useless information and pictures of dead bears. Pictures of dead bears, while great to look at, will not showcase to you different bear scat throughout the year, the different types of food sources bears find, and how to actually judge a decent bear. That is my goal: to pass along to you relevant, useful information about black-bear hunting that you can take to the field and find success. I have added plenty of pictures—as we all know, they speak a thousand words. I have also included some of my triumphs, mistakes, and hard-learned lessons to pass along the knowledge that I was both blessed to learn and cursed to find out.

I regret I did not start hunting bears when I was younger. I really didn't get into it until, by chance while deer hunting, I was able to score my first bear. I have been after bears now for several years with a pretty good success rate, but I sure would have loved to chase them in my teens. My stepson, Haydin, is very excited to get his hunting license next year, and he will be hunting bears with me come August 1, the good Lord willing.

By the time you finish reading this book, I hope you have gained some knowledge you didn't have before about hunting bears and that it provides not only entertainment but also years of hunting success and wonderful memories.

Like with any hunter who takes the sport seriously, I want to challenge each of you reading this book to try to become the best bear hunter you can be. Really study this book and bears. Get to know the difference between bear scat and other animal scat, be able to tell a grizzly print from that of a black bear, really understand how a bear thinks and why they do what they do. Be truly observant of the story that nature is trying to tell you as you walk through the woods, deserts, sage, swamps, or rugged mountain peaks. Be a black-bear hunter. You will not regret it. I know I don't.

Chapter One

Preseason Scouting

———

Your bear-hunting season is limited by the season's duration and available time. If if you have a family, your ability to go out and hunt during the season is probably very limited like mine is. That's why preseason scouting is a good way to maximize your hunt and increase your chances of tagging out. Plus, it helps get you in shape for the fun ahead!

Now, where I live, we have a fairly generous bear season from August 1 or August 15 to the middle of November, depending on which side of the Cascade Mountains you live on. But for those fellow bear hunters who live back East in Michigan, for instance, you have just over a month of a season for hunting, and it's a special draw. Scouting is especially important if you were drawn for a special permit. You don't want to let an opportunity like that go to waste because you didn't take the time to get out there and find a good hunting area.

Preseason scouting should start as early in the spring as possible. Bears usually come out of their dens in early April, depending on weather and your location. Scouting is a great way to dust off the hunting gear and ward off cabin fever. This effort should include getting yourself into hiking shape. You want to be able to hike where you need to and, provided the hunting gods smile upon you, carry out the bear as quickly as possible. Now personally, I do not work out a ton, as my day job is fairly physical. I walk a lot, lift heavy objects, and am generally active, but I don't hit the gym. I could stand to lose a few pounds, but that is just insulation in case I get cold out there. I have not had too many issues getting animals out from where I hunt, so at my current age of forty, I am not too worried

Sometimes you don't always find bears when scouting, but you might find an elk! This bull came in while I was waiting in a blueberry patch.

about it. Judge for yourself if you should skip that slice of pie and go for a quick hike instead. Of course, having some younger bucks in your hunting party doesn't hurt, as they are usually all too eager to carry something out, while us older and wiser hunters let them struggle. The point is, know your physical limits.

Getting in shape also depends on where you are hunting. If you are able to use your ATV or vehicle and cruise to where you want to hunt, set up a bait station, tree-stand hunt, and so on, you may not need to be in the best shape. But if you live where I live and pretty much everything is gated due to people trashing public and private hunting lands, then you are in for a hike . . . and the inevitable hike out. Make sure your boots are oiled and broken in before the first day of the season. A good waterproofing is likely necessary. Little things like having a good pair of boots that are broken in and easy to wear make a big difference. It is never any fun walking with a set of blisters on your heels reminding you of every step you take. I have been there enough times to know, and I don't want to go back. If you have the availability, take your backpack, fill it full of whatever you intend on bringing along then maybe a little extra, and go for a walk. Get your body used to lugging a full pack to make it easier once you start the season. Anything you can do to increase your strength, cardio, or lung capacity will help you in the long run in becoming a successful bear hunter.

On a side note, make sure your hunting vehicle is in good (or at least decent) running order. Get the oil changed, make sure your battery is in good shape, check the spare, and ensure you have a wheel lug wrench. Carry some basics with you, including fresh water, blankets, snacks, an emergency or first aid kit, some sort of fire starter, a small chainsaw for those unexpected spring storms, and the like. I always say, even if you are just going out for a day hike, make sure you pack enough supplies on your person to be able to stay the night out in the woods. You never know when you are going to roll an ankle, fall in a creek, or have nasty weather sock you in. Accidents happen, and most of the time you will not see it coming. The point is: be prepared.

Some early bear scouting, both in life and in season, never hurt anyone. Here is my hunting buddy Haydin enjoying some time out in the woods on a spring bear hunt.

Rule number one for bear hunting, which you will read throughout this book, is find what a bear is eating during that time of year specifically (berries, cambium, acorns, corn, fawns and calves—whatever it may be) with minimal human interference and you will likely find bears. This is the absolute golden rule with bears. Stick this in your head, refer to it when you are out in the woods, and along with a bit of luck you will spot bears. Of course, this doesn't count for baiting bears, but that's a different story we will deal with in a later chapter. Preseason scouting is a great time to hone your future hunting efforts. Bring a digital camera if you can. It can help make you familiar with some of the sites you have visited, you can take photos of sign to compare later, and so forth. I usually carry a small digital camera just big enough to fit into my front pocket or coat pocket. Remember, if you are putting it in your coat, put it in a pocket with a zipper—they can fall out while you are hiking about. This kind of reveals my age a bit, I guess, as most people have cell phones with cameras on them. I, for some reason, actually use a camera instead of my cell phone.

With the price of gas nowadays and the amazing technology we have at the tips of our fingers, Google Earth is a wonderful tool when scouting for bears, or any other big-game animal, for that matter. If you are not familiar with this program for your computer, get to know it. It essentially gives you a bird's eye view of anywhere in the world from altitude down to street level on certain parts of the map. It's a bit scary actually to think that this is the technology they are showing us, but put on your tinfoil hat and start checking it out. We cannot stop Google, so you might as well embrace it.

I owe my 2009 spring bear success, in part, to the use of this piece of technology. I was in search of bear sign in a wonderful area called Sultan, which is at the foot of a mountain pass called Stevens Pass. Surrounded by massive rocky peaks covered with snow, the jagged mountains seem to tear at the sky in utter defiance of time. I love this area for bears—not just for the beauty of the land but also the bounty of bears in the area. It is filled with wooded areas, clear cuts of various stages of growth, creeks, ponds, hills, and some of the thickest, nastiest brush you will want to tromp through. Perfect!

While walking along, I happened upon a pile of bear scat just on the edge of a group of trees that were about ten years old. I worked my way deeper into the thick brush, which was choking the trees, and found

An example of bear poo in spring, when the bear has been busy eating grass. It almost looks like horse droppings.

more scat. Tangled among the trees were blackberries and devil's club, a particularly nasty creation with thorns all over. Picture the scene in the classic Disney movie *Sleeping Beauty*, during which the prince has to cut his way through the magical growing spiked vines—it was about like that except without the sword. This is where a good pair of leather work gloves come in handy. I hardly ever go bear hunting without some plain old leather gloves. Now, this little bit of sign was just what I was looking for during this special draw hunt. It was a starting point—it was enough.

I pushed through some more brush and ended up stumbling upon small openings in the thicket, which were actually caused by dead Douglas fir trees that had been stripped by bears for their cambium layer. They die completely within two years of being stripped, generally, and then this allows more sunlight to filter through to the grass below, a great find for early spring. The area didn't offer much room to hunt, as the opening was very limited.

Not knowing much about the area and having decided it was too thick (in the patch I was in, I had about ten yards of visibility), I backed out and went home. It would not have been much fun to try to line up a shot

Get to know your scat. This is not from a bear but from a coyote. You will see lots of hair and small bits of bone in coyote scat. Not to mention it is generally smaller than any bear worth interest to you.

with my 3 × 9 Leupold scope in such close quarters. Later that night, I looked that area up on Google Earth. I noticed that there were small pockets of open area scattered all throughout this half-mile-by-half-mile bean-shaped area. Even better, on one side of this area, lined by mature trees, was a larger area about half the size of a football field. This clearing butted up against a steep wooded hillside. I would have to check this out! So, off I went on my next hunt to check out my newfound glimmer of hope.

Come to find out, it was a slightly swampy area but covered in nice green grass (a staple

Bears will strip the bark off Douglas fir and other pine trees to reach the cambium layer during the spring. This generally kills the tree the following year.

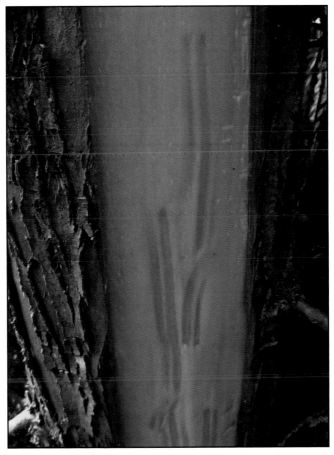

Pay special attention to a tree with vertical teeth marks left by a bear. Once the bark is stripped, a bear scrapes its teeth against the wood, which leaves these marks.

for bears in the spring) and lined with perfect trees that bears like to peel this time of year. More importantly, and to the point, I had to travel through about fifty yards of thick blackberry brush before I was able to access the openings. The average hunter would walk right by it not realizing it was an absolute bearadise (yes, a bear paradise) on the other side of the brush. I call it bearadise because it had food, cover, and an enormous amount of bear sign, including recently damaged trees and scat. I was later able to bag a nice boar out of this very spot from about fifty yards thanks to the use of my computer and field verification. A little bit of luck and persistence didn't hurt either.

Again, take a close look at trees for these vertical teeth marks. Porcupines damage trees, too, but they usually go farther up onto the tree and will often leave quills near the base of the tree; the scratch marks are narrower, too. Porcupine scat will be small round balls that almost look like owl pellets in size and shape (they don't have mouse fur in them like owl pellets do). Don't confuse a deer or elk rub for a bear peel, either. Just be observant and study the pictures, and you will be able to tell the differences between them in no time.

You see, it doesn't matter if you are in the thick forests of Maine, the vast canyons of Alaska, or the rain-soaked coasts of Washington, the formula for success is finding bear food for that particular time of year (and, of course, bear habitat). You need to ask yourself, what are they eating in your area at that specific time? Are you doing a spring, summer, fall, or winter hunt? Depending on where you live, there will be different food sources from old apple trees to a farmer's corn field to vast blueberry fields high in the mountains to flowing green seas of grass that line a saltwater flat bordering the vast Pacific Ocean. East Coast hunters should be looking for acorns and other nuts available. Anything the bear can eat readily to put weight on for winter is what you must concentrate on when scouting. Remember food sources as your main thought because that is a bear's main thought unless it is the bear rut.

You can tell the difference between fresh damage and old bear damage fairly quickly on stripped trees. Notice the sap running down the tree. The tree will also turn yellow, orange, red, and then finally lose all needles or leaves. Even if all you find is older damage, the area still might be worth looking into for bear activity. Search the area more closely for further sign.

If you are having trouble finding out what the heck bears eat in your neck of the woods, check out your state's hunting forums online, and simply ask around. There are several bear forums available, as well as numerous forums online dedicated to bear hunting in general. Don't just hop on a forum, ask for a secret spot (or any spot, for that matter), and expect results. Put in your time with the forum by contributing and you will have much better luck. *Bear Hunting Magazine* is a helpful periodical to pick up for some light reading and to get the beginning bear hunter some basic knowledge. My point is, take the time and effort to expand your knowledge not just by reading this book but also by researching online, watching YouTube videos on bear hunting, and getting out into the wild and looking for signs of your prey. Bears will eat just about anything . . . ask any game-camera owner who has put his camera up in bear country. If you are finding sign but no bears, don't get too frustrated. I see it far too often online where people will find sign and then get frustrated. Give yourself some time to find bears, and give yourself some credit for finding bear sign. Remember, if you find fresh sign, you are on the right track. Just stick with it.

I am going to start you off with the idea of a spring bear hunt. Not many states have spring bear hunts permits available for just anyone to purchase over the counter. Idaho has them; in my state of Washington, it is a special draw. Make absolutely sure you check your game regulations before heading out to hunt. Know the rules to play by.

You can see in this picture that a bear was working the side of the road for tasty cambium from the tree on the left. Keep your eyes peeled (no pun intended) for such obvious signs.

So, in the spring, what is there to eat in the wild? Winter has lost its grip and snow is melting or has melted. Nature is greening up, which is your first clue. Bears will eat fresh shoots of grass and plants, so keep an eye out for any area that will green up faster than others. For example, clearings in trees, old logging roads, southern exposure of hillsides, swamp edges, tidal flats, and the like. Areas that green up first will naturally attract animals of all sorts, bears included. The plant matter helps to kick-start the bear's digestive system. You will sometimes hear people refer to a bear losing its "plug," a term used for, well, a plug that the bear acquires in its intestines during hibernation. After they emerge from their dens and begin foraging, they soon eliminate this blockage and their stomach begins working normally again.

If an area has logging operations in progress, oftentimes you can check in with the logging office or loggers themselves and ask where they have seen bear activity either in the current year or years past. I have generally found loggers to be a wealth of information as far as bear location is concerned. Check with local farmers or people who may have crop or livestock damage due to bears. They are out on their tractors long hours and might have spotted a nice black bear that just isn't welcome on the farm. After you have checked the forums, farmers, loggers, and even

Bear scat can tell you a lot about the local bears. Check out any piles you may come across and inspect for freshness and what they have been eating. Notice how fresh the wetter of these two piles looks? This is usually a great sign that a bear is in the area or was not too long ago. Step on the piles to mark that you have already checked them out. That way if you come down that path again and piles have not been stepped on, you know they are fresh from the last time through.

your local wildlife agent, you should have a general idea of where to start. If not, really focus on south-facing slopes and anywhere that is greening up with vegetation. Take a drive or a hike and look for yourself. Put in the time! Watch the sides of trails and roads you walk. Check for scat in any sort of green grass opening in the woods or on hillsides.

Bears are naturally lazy. They plod along looking for the easiest meal they can get. They also like to remain cool. Although this isn't a big deal in the spring, in the summer and early fall always keep an eye out for remote creeks or nice brushy draws. Even in the desert where bears are located, check rambling creek beds and draws—you'll be surprised how often you will find bear sign in places like this. In mountainous territory, keep an eye on avalanche chutes. In the winter, an avalanche may have occurred and killed some animals. This might have pushed food down the hill or onto the hillside. Bears will smell this and come to gnaw on the remains. Try to think outside the box. Working avalanche chutes, you might come into contact with a wolverine, too, which is always a treat.

In springtime, focus on what there is to eat because it is limited compared to the summer. In later spring, doe deer and cow elk will start to drop their fawns and calves. Believe it or not, these are tasty snacks for bears, coyotes, cougars, and other wild predators. So, in your travels, if you happen to find areas where you know fawns and calves are birthed or hidden, pay special attention. There is a specific hill where I go archery elk hunting on which I have seen several cow elk dropping calves, and I have often seen bears strolling along looking for tasty baby treats. It's not a nice thing to think about, but nature isn't nice. It is not a Disney movie, as most hunters are well aware. If you have ever seen an animal get killed by another, it is generally a pretty nasty way to go.

I like to keep a small tablet with me to write down notes about where I have found bear signs, the time of month, what type of sign (scat, tracks, damage, animal kills), what is growing where, and the specific dates. These can be a handy in later seasons to remind you of spots that used to hold bears and spots that, given a few years, may hold bears. For example, if I come across a fresh clear-cut, it usually will not be much good for about three years. But by then, it should start to become a place I want to check out. This is because it takes a bit of time for brush to come back. But once it does, the bears (deer, elk, and so forth) love it. As hunters, we truly should thank the logging industry and support them all we can since logging can produce such great habitat for animals of all sorts.

The same can be said wherever you may be hunting. Did you come across an old apple orchard or old homestead with twisted fruit trees on them that are not bearing fruit yet but will be a bit later? Mark it on a GPS if available and come back later in the year (or just plain remember where it is). This could also help out with your deer season, if you hunt those animals like I do. Is there a small water spring with grass and brush

Yellow, orange, and red dying trees are bright call signs to the bear hunter. Notice on this hillside all the dying trees, which were getting hammered by bears for the past few years in spring. This should indicate to you that you must check out this area. If it is too thick to spot and stalk, get up high and call into it with a predator call.

around it in the desert, an elk wallow, or other likely area for game? Mark it down! Soon you will have a good collection of notes and places to check. Get organized with spots and signs and you might be surprised about how successful you will be with this added knowledge.

As you hunt or hike looking for bears, you'll notice that their scat changes noticeably throughout the seasons depending on what they're eating. In early spring, bear scat is almost always plant matter. In the later spring, when fruits and berries start to arrive, the scat will have various shades of purple or bluish red and plenty of seeds in it. Later on in the year, it will become more berrylike, have chunks of apples in it, corn, or any other types of fruit or vegetables available to eat, or it might be a darker color from the meat the bear is scavenging.

In the spring as you scout, pay special attention to berry plants that are in bloom. Take the time to get to know native plants and what to look for—plants that bear fruit and nuts are key. These could be great spots to revisit later in the year once the fruits are in full swing. If you

Another example of bear scat. Once you really get into bear hunting, you will find yourself stopping and checking out bear scat every time you find it. At least I know I do.

have hills or mountains where you are hunting, walk the ridgelines and look carefully at any game trails you come along. Be observant of your surroundings. Pay special attention in the spring to any brush or saplings that look busted up or otherwise freshly thrashed upon. While this could be a simple case of a deer or elk—or cows for that matter—grazing on it, it could also be a bear marking its territory. Examine the plants and look for any residual hairs on them that might have been left from the bear. It is common for a bear to rub its back against a sapling, bend it over its shoulder, and bite or break it off: just a general bear announcement to other bears in the area that this is its territory.

Here a bear decided to mark its territory. Ask yourself if the leaves are wilted or still in good shape. This will give you a hint of how fresh it is. Are there other trees or bushes like this in the area? By doing a little investigating, you might just find a big old bruin marking his home range!

Nature is trying to tell you something. Stop and listen. Inspect why this bush's leaves are turned upside down and why branches are busted on it. This was caused by a bear, as the hair found on it later proved. It was eating the berries.

Keep in mind, too, that not all berries and fruits arrive at the same time, and sometimes it even depends on elevation. Lower-elevation fruit might ripen quicker than fruit at higher elevation. Pay close attention to this detail. Learn when fruit, berries, and nuts will be ready to eat and at what elevation. If a bunch of berries are ripe down low, say in July, and your season doesn't start until August, those berries might be done by the start of season

While the fruit is not ready to eat yet, this bush will soon be a wonderful food source for bears. Get to know the local plants in your hunting area, what they look like, and what they produce. This knowledge will greatly increase your chances of narrowing down a food source for bears throughout the year.

at that elevation. Therefore, you may need to go higher or find another food source. Really take the time to get to know what is growing in your area. I cannot say that enough—get to know what is growing in your area, and when it is ripe, you have just simplified your bear hunting by 50 percent. It is like baiting the natural way.

Personally, I like to find creek bottoms that I know have brush in them along with mature timber and older clear-cuts. For the western states this is my general plan. In contrast, on the eastern part of Washington, we have a lot of desert with rolling ancient volcanic hills. These hills are covered in mesquite and sage brush and dotted with lots of pine trees that range from a lone tree to a whole massive forest. Most of the brush is confined to creek bottoms or anywhere there is water, which is limited. Elk and mule deer roam freely while some white-tailed deer walk like ghosts along creek and river bottoms. Bears on this side of the mountains again head for the cooler draws and brush-choked creeks. Any place with water, brush, and little human interaction is a great place to start looking for desert bears, or bears in general, during hot summer days. They like to be cool, so remember these spots. If you find a stand of prickly pears in the desert, make sure to keep an eye on it when the season comes around. *Bears love some prickly pears!*

We have lovely majestic mountains and volcanoes where I live. One such volcano is Mount Baker, a great area for bears, and it really calls out to the spirit of any hunter who gets to bask in its glory. For any mountainous terrain, I like to find mountain blueberry fields or high alpine grassy fields. You will find bears up top later in the season scarfing down blueberries to pack on the pounds before winter finally hits. Grab some United States Forest Service (USFS) maps and explore what your state has to offer. Also, keep an eye on trailhead signs. Often hikers will post on the signs "BEAR SEEN AT [SUCH AND SUCH] LOCATION." You can use this to your advantage. Don't be afraid to check hiker forums online, as well. Hikers often do your scouting for you. Just remember to share the trail. I always like to give a smile and say hello if I am on a trail that is being used by other hikers. A little hunter diplomacy can go a long way.

There is a reason they call it hunting and not target practice or grocery shopping. Work is involved, and no amount of reading books or watching hunting videos can compete with actually getting out there and being a part of nature, as humans are born to be. You're a hunter by design, there is no denying that. Even nonhunters are designed this

In mountainous regions across the Northwest, there are endless miles of blueberry fields, which are prime bear habitat.

way—despite how much they may try to banish the thought of earning their food instead of buying it at a grocery store. If you want some non-GMO, gluten-free, free-range, cage-free, grass-fed meat . . . go hunt!

In the preseason, if you get the chance, you can use pruners to trim back brush that leads to a certain water hole or possible feeding area—say, an old fruit orchard or other tree-stand area that offers fruit. If you take the time early in the year to clear a path, animals of all types will start to use it. By the time the season comes, this could make your approach to the feeding area much more concealed or allow you to set up a blind or stand. My point is, if it is really thick where you live, that's great for bears! Don't let that discourage your hunting—it just might make it better. Clear a path, bears will start to use it, and now you can manipulate the situation to your benefit. Lead the path to a choke point, a logjam, a watering hole in hot climates, past your tree stand—anything to give you that edge. When stalking, you will need all the help you can get. And remember, you will blow stalks, but you are supposed to. Cougars don't have 100 percent success rates when hunting, why should you? That is how you learn, and it teaches patience. Don't get discouraged if you live in an area that is thick

Two-week-old scat (my best guess)—notice the berries on the ground and in the scat. This was in the fall in Alaska. There is an obvious difference between bear scat in spring, summer, and fall. Notice how one is mainly of grass (spring), summer scat contains harvest berry seeds and is berry colored (blackberries), and fall is that of late-blooming forest floor small red berries. The key point here is that scat holds the food sources available at that time of year, which change as the seasons change. So, if you find scat that is fresh, it should help you decipher just what the bears are into at that moment.

I know when my brothers, father, and hunting buddies started hunting elk in a specific area, we really didn't know it that well. We would be in elk for the first few days, but then they would disappear for a while and we wouldn't know where to look. However, through the years, with careful observation, many failures, some successes, and a ton of scouting and glassing, we have really pinpointed where the elk are during the season. We know where they go when they get blown out of the valley. We know the escape routes, wallows, where they feed in the morning, where they bed midday, and where they will come out at night.

Bears are a little tougher to narrow down because they are not herd animals, but you could imagine how incredible and scary that would be to see a herd of bears grazing along some mountainside. The point is, the

Blossoms turn to fruit or berries. Now where there used to be pretty white flowers, there are wonderful, juicy bear treats. Find food, find bears!

more time you hunt and get to know an area, the better hunter you will be in that area.

When you are out scouting, do not just pass areas because they are close to a road or human activity. The bearadise I referred to earlier is actually an area not too far from where you have to park to get into the area. It is maybe a half mile in, but people walk right by it because it is so close to where you have to park. They never realize they just passed up a great spot for bears, coyotes, bobcats, and deer.

Another topic I want to touch on is your gear. Use what you have available. You do not need to have the newest of the new, the best of the best, and the latest camo pattern. Ever see those old pictures of men with elk or deer (or even bears) piled onto the hoods of their vehicles or hanging from a tree? Were they decked out in all X brand of camo? No, they had on whatever they had available. Now, modern gear is definitely nice to have, especially with all the advancements in waterproofing, which makes items lighter and life easier. But I know plenty of people who go out looking for bears in their blue jeans and T-shirts in the summer, and they do just fine.

In late May to June, you will find black bears in heat looking for a mate. The bear rut . . . yes, bears have a rut. Boars will be out cruising and looking for the scent of a female in heat. This is a great time to look for bears in your area. If you have any sort of road system in the hunting area, try to get above them and watch the roads, which provide easy walking for the boys, so this is where you will find them. If you don't have roads, watch any sort of clearing, especially open fields or meadows with tree lines. Boars will wander all over looking for a receptive females, so it is a perfect time to spot bears or just get used to spotting bears. If you do spot a bear, don't think he will stick around there forever. It will be unlikely that the big boar you spot will be in the exact area a month or two down the road once the season starts, but at least you know the bear was there and what it looks like. It could be a good place to start your hunt depending on food in the area.

The potent-smelling skunk cabbage comes up in spring to offer a meager meal for bears. They tend to eat the roots and leaves of the plant. You will find the yellow flowers shown here coming up first, then you will see the large lettuce-like leaves. If you smack them with a stick and you smell skunk, you've got some skunk cabbage.

I just did a little bit of scouting this past weekend (as it is the end of July as I write this). Our general bear season starts August 1, so I was trying to find some new areas. During 2015 in Washington, the weather was very hot and very dry. Much of the land normally open to hunting will be closed until we get a bit more rain due to the fire danger. However, I wanted to go check a few spots out, regardless. Plus, it was raining when I went out, which was a nice change.

While hiking, always be on the lookout for food sources for bears. Huckleberries make a delicious snack while searching for bears.

If you find a pile like this, you are closing in. Walk slowly, watch your wind, and listen closely as you travel. You could be very close to a bear.

As I entered the area, it was hilly and treed, which is typical for our neck of the woods. The new Douglas firs were about four years old or so when I entered the gated area. A fresh clear-cut lined the ridgetop, and mature trees dominated the area. Having never been in this area before, I decided to just follow what I thought looked good. I followed the road through some cool mature trees with a nice creek bed that cut downhill toward a lake. As I came out of the mature trees, I headed uphill for quite some time.

After I arrived at the ridgetop, sweating a bit, the rain decided to increase and cool me off, as well as to keep the mosquitos at bay—both of which I was thankful for. Mosquitos seem to love me. Anyway, I had been noticing some bear scat, which was fairly fresh, as I got closer and closer to the top of the ridge. A bear had been working the area. I had assumed it was a boar or sow without cubs, as most of the scat was equal in size, which made me assume it was from the same or a similar-sized bear. Nothing huge but definitely worth checking out. I then decided to take the road less travelled, literally.

It was an older logging road, overgrown slightly with yet another great bear area on either side. It was thick with brush—berries of various kinds, some with fruit, some with unripe fruit, and some brush that had already dropped its fruit. What did I discover in the area? Water, food, and cover, as well as area for the bears to roam. All good things. This was further confirmed by some damage to blackberry bushes that I had assumed was caused by a bear, although I couldn't find any hair on that particular bush. It appeared to me that the bear stood on its hind legs, pulled the bundle of berries down to it, and snapped the branch. The leaves were still green but wilting, which led me to believe it happened within two or three days.

Taking my sweet time to walk down the road and observe, I noticed several stumps had been ripped into. Some stumps had older damage, while others were just recently damaged. Most of the stumps I had observed were surrounded with grass on the edge of the brush. I was looking for a spot with thorny blackberry bushes to show me what color bear might be working the area and to confirm it was fairly fresh. As I saw more and more sign, it occurred to me that hunting, or scouting, is very similar to criminal forensic science. Nature, like a crime scene, will tell a story to those willing to listen or decipher the clues left behind. It can be from animal prints, hair left at the scene of a rub, scat, sets of tracks chasing each other, and so forth. Think of this when scouting, and be sure to take your time looking at what nature is trying to tell you.

Bears will tear into all sorts of stumps looking for tasty grubs or ants. As you walk around, train your eyes to watch for such obvious yet easily missed signs of bear activity. Notice the stump with only a little damage to it (the bark torn off and some digging) and that the damage was not extensive. Plus, the bark is freshly torn off, as we can tell by the color of the bark that was against the stump, how moist it was, and the color of the bark. Did I interrupt the bear, or was there not enough food in the stump to continue digging?

The older road I was on came to a dead end that had a game trail on it. Bears enjoy traveling on roads or trails just like people do because it is an easy way to travel. Remember this, easy travel means fewer calories burned, which means more fat retained and an easier hibernation. Still walking the same road, I was noticing more sign from a bear that I had missed before because now I was facing the opposite direction and able to see things from a different angle. Sometimes you just need a new perspective.

Here is another example of what to look for on a torn-up stump. The stump was obviously infested with insects that the bear got to eat. Not all torn stumps are fresh, mind you. Do you still see insects running about in disarray? Or has the colony long been abandoned? How does the torn wood look? Is it weathered from exposure or does it look like it remained darker in color? Are there plants growing over and through the torn remnants of the stump? Do leaves and needles cover the torn wood, or is it clear of other foreign objects? If it is clear of other debris, it is likely fresh. If leaves and needles or other wind-blown debris cover it, it is likely older.

This new perspective allowed me to see what I had missed on the way in—such as a couple of game trails, which were what I like to call bear tunnels. The terrain where I hunt is often so thick that a bear, or sometimes deer, will literally have a tunnel they travel through, which is probably why we call bears "brush pigs" sometimes around these parts. Bears are more likely the creators of these tunnels because of the low height of the tunnel and how it is bored out. I have seen deer get very low, and I have even seen white-tailed deer get on their knees to soldier-crawl out of an area to avoid detection. Again, though, this is a preseason sign to check. It is likely if you are hunting a thick area and there is a tunnel close to the ground that is larger than what a coyote would use that it could be from a bear. Check any surrounding brush or thorns for hair to confirm your suspicions.

Bear habitats are often very thick. So thick, in fact, that bears will make tunnels through the brush, as you can faintly see here (though the tunnel is actually bigger than it looks in the picture). Check these tunnels and any thorns nearby for the presence of black-bear hair. If you find some, you'll know you are on the right track.

After I got back to the main road, I decided to walk it a bit farther. One side of the road were tall, majestic Douglas fir trees mixed with mighty cedars, and on the other side was more thick brush and smaller pine trees. It was a bit thick to hunt but a good spot to try to spot a bear feeding. As I walked down the road, I spotted another stump that had been torn into by what I believed to be a bear. This was very fresh—it probably happened within the past few hours. I say this as there

In this picture, close inspection of the area around a torn up stump revealed what tore into it. If you look closely, you can see the black-bear's hair on the thorns. This also tells us that the bear working the area is a standard black color and not a color-phase bear. However, that does not mean a coveted color-phase bear or a black bear with a great white chevron blaze on its chest isn't close by!

were still bugs scurrying around on the stump that were not happy their home was ripped up. This stump was bordered by blackberries, and you could see where the animal had pushed down the grass and gotten into the brush a bit while tearing into the stump. This was a good spot to try to find what was doing this and what color it may be. Sure enough, after a few seconds of searching, I found a couple long black bear hairs. This told me that at least one bear in the area is your standard black bear, not a bear in a color phase. Some hunters may really want a color-phase bear. Finding these hairs may have them thinking they should move on from the area. While this might be understandable, I have found there is usually more than one bear working an area. If there is one, there is likely another.

Using little tricks, such as searching for hairs in briars or along game trails, setting up game cameras throughout an area you want to hunt, and just generally walking or driving around to get to know the area, can greatly increase your chances of success. Really take the time, slow yourself down, and be observant. I know it is difficult for many of us to be able to slow down. I sometimes have to remind myself to do that. "Walk slower—I am hunting, I am not in a rush," I tell myself. Highly caffeinated, often rushed, and living a hectic, instant-gratification lifestyle can be detrimental to methodical, slow-paced tracking or scouting.

On my way out of this area, I plodded along keeping mental notes of where I saw sign so when I returned I would be able to identify where the sign was. I will often step in or kick bear scat as I go along so when I return I know what is fresh from the last visit. I also noticed that on the way out I found some older bear scat next to some fresh scat from this spring. It was full of grass, dried out, and had turned a darker black. This told me that at least one bear was working the area during the springtime, too. All in all, it was not a bad trip.

Now for the sake of argument, let us say that I head back to this spot just before the season or even during the season. Say I find bigger scat in diameter than the previous sets of scat, and I know it has been left since my last visit because I smashed down the other piles of scat. This would likely be another bear—possibly a bigger one than the average bear I estimate the first one to be. Since it has been so dry, any water holes in the area would be a great place to check for tracks or to set up and watch. Bears like to cool down as much as the next animal.

Scouting for bears does not have to be limited to preseason, either. I was deer hunting in the 2015 season, and my hunting buddies and family came upon a cool site. There was a pullout along an old logging road, which looked out over a brushy creek bottom in an otherwise burned-out forest. There were several piles of about two weeks to month-old scat everywhere. I think we counted thirty-plus piles. Most of these contained rose hip seeds, a local bear favorite. Keep in mind, this

The thirty-eight piles scattered around in this photo are all about two weeks old or older. While the bear has moved on, his food source, rose hips, will still be here next year. Perhaps if I come back a month earlier next year, I might score a bear out of this area. Remember to keep track of where you find sign and how old it is. It can save a lot of walking and wasted energy the next season.

took place in eastern Washington, a much drier, hotter area than western Washington. I had already tagged out on deer, so I was curious about all this older bear sign.

This is the additive to all those bear piles: rose hips. While not edible for humans (unless you want to hallucinate and have diarrhea), bears sure seem to enjoy them.

It was obvious the bear was working the area rose hips and likely had a bed nearby. My boy and I looked around but didn't find the bear. We did, however, come upon a beehive that the bear recently dug up and feasted on. The bear was likely around, but I didn't see him that day. What did this tell me? Well, the fruit was gone from most of the rose hips, so the majority of the food source was gone. But it also told me that next season, if I want to go bear hunting, I need to head over to that area a month or so before deer season, as it is likely that the rose hips will ripen and the bear (or another bear) will be hitting that area, which had food, cover, and water. You see where I am coming from on this? Even if you find old scat, particularly scat that is only a few weeks old, you can pinpoint when you should revisit the area in the next season. Keep an eye out for places like this, and you will be one step ahead next season!

Chapter Two

Weapons and Shot Placement

When it comes to bears in comparison to deer, it can be said that they are both very difficult animals. Both can run great distances if wounded. Both can hurt you if cornered. My observations have led me to believe that bear and deer handle getting wounded differently, though. Deer, when shot, usually head away from the area as quickly as possible—sometimes to cover, sometimes just to get as much distance from the area as possible. Bears, on the other hand, seem to head straight for cover. Thick, dark, nasty cover. The type of cover you normally wouldn't want to go in, let alone go in after a wounded bear. In addition, they might bury themselves into a logjam like a thirsty tick on the side of an elk or any other defensive position they can find in the cover. Thus, in my opinion, bears command a certain amount of respect—no, that's not the word I'm looking for . . . they arouse *fear* more than a deer does. Bears are quick, vicious predators that have absolute superior strength, agility, endurance, and smelling ability over humans, without question. Not to mention they can be very aggressive—add into the mix being wounded, cornered, or desperate and you have a recipe for trouble. These are all very good reasons to know when to shoot at a bear (and more important when *not* to) and make sure you are using a weapon that has proper take-down ability. Let's discuss these options in this chapter.

COMPOUND BOWS

I once was asked by a nonhunting friend if a bow could take down a bear. He didn't realize that I hunt bears with a bow at times but more important for my point, I hunt elk (a larger animal than a bear) with my bow every season. He was astounded that a bow and arrow could take down an elk or bear. I explained (as you probably already know if you hunt) that shot placement is absolutely everything. If you double-lung shoot an animal properly with an arrow, that animal is not going far before it drowns in blood. The same principle is true for bears with a few variables.

I mainly use a compound bow when I go bow hunting. I started using a bow back in 1994—an old Fred Bear brand that I bought off a coworker's kid. It had small cams by today's standards, no peep sight, three sight pins (twenty, thirty, and forty yards, respectively), and I pulled the string back with my fingers with no trigger release. I also didn't have any sort of range finder. I was an oil-refinery worker fresh out of high school, so I kept it basic. I spent many days that summer practicing with my buddy, from whom I bought it; he gave me some pointers on how to aim, hold the bow, and so on. It was a carefree time, which I look back on fondly. I truly believe becoming a bow hunter made me a better hunter overall.

That first deer season I used a bow (which started the beginning of September) I was blessed to take a 3 × 2 blacktail deer (that's a five-pointer for you hunters east of the Mississippi) at about thirty-five yards. Clean pass, double lung, and the deer went about ten yards. The bow I used was pretty archaic compared to the blazing-hot compound bows of today. But it got the job done. Why? Shot placement and a bit of luck. If you study the anatomy of your prey and are able to decipher how to quickly kill the animal with the least amount of pain or suffering, not only will you become a better hunter, but you will also work less. Additionally, the bear, or any animal we kill as hunters, deserves a quick, humane dispatch. Do your part to ensure it happens that way. Do not be afraid to pass on a shot. You will not regret passing on a questionable shot when it comes down to it. It is far better to pass a shot than to wound an animal and possibly never recover it.

Back then, my broad heads were little more than box cutter blades attached to the arrowhead. Today, I use 100-grain solid steel Montec G5 broad heads. There are various brands of various styles of broad heads available today. If you are a bow hunter, you need to find an arrow that flies well, is consistently accurate, and devastates your prey. Much like with bullets and a rifle, find an arrowhead that shoots well from your bow and for your style. Don't be afraid to buy a few different brands of broad heads to see how they fly for you. Montecs have worked well for me, so I stick with them both for big game and with a small-game arrowhead. If it isn't broke . . . well, you know the rest.

On this subject, I would recommend using solid broad heads for bears instead of mechanical broad heads. Bears are muscular, thick, tough animals with longer hair than deer or elk for the most part. Fat and hair quickly plug wounds on bears, which makes them notoriously hard to track. One basic reason is that if something is mechanical, it can and will eventually fail. If something is just a solid blade, that is one less thing that can go wrong. I am not saying that modern mechanical arrowheads are junk or fail often; I am simply stating I would personally prefer not to use them for bears. I have seen what mechanical broad heads do to deer and bobcats, and they are devastating, but those animals are not bears.

Mechanical broad heads work well for some applications, but I would pass on using them for black bears. Bears have thick shoulder muscles and shoulder-blade bones. When the mechanical broad head is released and smashes into the bear's thick hair and hide, the blades begin to spread out. That thick hide and hair can act like a vest of protection for the animal and cause the arrow to lose much of its energy so a complete pass through is difficult. When a mechanical arrowhead hits a deer, the fur is generally shorter than a bear's and not as dense. This allows the arrow to retain more of its energy than when it hits a bear. Therefore, mechanicals would be more efficient on deer than bears, in my humble opinion. But, again, I encourage you to find the combination that works well for you and your setup.

If you are new to bow hunting, the term "draw weight" is used to measure the amount of poundage a person must draw back to get the bow to the fully drawn position. The draw weight for my bow is set at seventy pounds, so I basically have to lift about seventy pounds all the way back with my one arm until I get to a let-off position. Well, not entirely, as my left arm holding the bow does take some of the strain. Once a person is fully drawn with a compound bow, the draw weight can be reduced greatly from the initial draw weight depending on the bow setting. That draw weight setting works for me. But if you are new to bow hunting, you need to find a draw weight that fits you and your individual strength. The more draw weight, the more energy the arrow will have. Of course, the more draw weight also means it will be harder to pull back and retain a pulled back position. With practice, you will become more and more accustomed to it, and pulling back on the bow will not be as hard as when you initially tried it. You need to practice as much as possible with your bow before the season to become an accurate shot and get your chest and arms in shape for the draw back.

If you have never hunted with a bow before, go down to your local outdoor shop or family archery store. They will be able to walk you through all you need to know about your draw length, what weight you will need the bow set at, and what weight it legally needs to be set at in your state. States also have rules on how much your arrow shaft and head weight combined can be, which is usually around 300 grains in total weight. Make sure to check your regulations thoroughly before heading out into the bush after a bear. If you are unsure about something, ask your local game department about it and learn from it. We are all beginners at one point in time. A state will also usually have a limit on how much let off you are allowed, so be sure your bow meets those requirements, as well.

There are numerous brands of bows from which to choose. Hoyt, Mathews, Bear, Bowtech, and so on are brand names. You will find the typical fan boys (or girls) for any particular brand you happen to pick, just like some prefer Chevy or Ford, while others prefer Toyota. The key is to try out some different styles of bow and see which one best suits you and your budget. Most of my brothers and my Dad shoot Mathews brand. My current Hoyt bow is a hand-me-down from my younger brother (isn't that a hand-me-up?). I can honestly say I have killed many more animals with it in my hands than in my brother's, so I have that over him. It is an older bow without a ton of bells and whistles on it, but it gets the job done, and that works for me. I don't see a reason to go out and spend six hundred dollars or more on a new bow when this ole bow has treated me well and doesn't cost a dime. Plus, it fit my budget at the time I got it—free! It's hard to argue with free. I have no reason to want or need another bow for the present time— even though I get a razzing for having an older bow in camp. Of course, it is hard to argue with results.

My current setup for my sight pins (pins that are attached to the front of the bow, which are set for different yardage) is twenty, thirty, forty, and fifty yards, respectively. Almost all of my shots at an animal with the bow have been thirty yards or less and are usually closer to twenty yards or less. My closest shot has been about three yards at a white-tailed doe that was on the other side of a tree from me at ground level; she went nowhere. Some will say I need more pins for twenty-five, thirty-five, and forty-five yards. Others might suggest I have too many already. It really depends on how you hunt and the territory you are hunting. I don't like taking shots out to fifty yards on an animal—not because I cannot make them but because that leaves a greater margin for error. The animal may react to the sound of your bow, duck down, or so on. There might be a twig you didn't see that deflects the arrow. There is also a greater chance for wind to affect the arrow depending on conditions. The farther away something is, the more likely something could go wrong—it's as simple as that. The closer the better, I say.

I like to get as close as I can to an animal, but I like having the option of sending an arrow out to fifty yards in case the animal has been shot, runs a short distance, and then looks back to give me a chance at another shot. Then I know I can send another arrow toward the animal at a slightly greater distance with the hope of sealing the deal. You will also find that KISS works—Keep It Simple, Stupid. If I don't have a Christmas tree of pins to look at and I only have five to worry about, I am less likely to focus so much on figuring out which pin I need and instead focus on my distance, breathing, lining up the shot, and ensuring there isn't some tricky twig I didn't see that will send my arrow sailing off to never-never land. If I need to take a twenty-five or thirty-five yard shot, I just aim with my pins between

As a bow hunter, you already know the importance of finding your arrow, which can tell you a lot about where you possibly hit the animal. For example, if blood runs all the way down the arrow and onto the fletching, you know you have a complete pass through of the arrow. Bubbles in the blood are a good sign, too, as they usually mean a lung shot. If you find the arrow is broken, which end did you find? Is the arrowhead still in the animal to cause damage? Did you find the busted fletching end, and if so, is there blood on the fletching or not? If there isn't, the arrow did not pass through the animal. Study your arrow once you find it, as it has a story to tell and might give insight on how to track the bear.

the area on the animal I want to hit. Aim small, miss small. Focus your aim not at the whole side of the bear but, say, just behind the shoulder blade near its armpit. Pick a small spot on the bear and try to hit it.

You may want to consider, particularly if you are going for an extended bow-hunting backpacking trip, bringing along a bow repair kit. Generally, the kit will come with some basic tools you may need—Allen-head wrenches and so on—maybe a few extra pins, and the like. Do not forget to wax down your bowstring periodically, as well. Waxing your bowstring adds life to the string, allows it to retain its strength, and prevents it from becoming frayed. If your bowstring starts to show signs of excessive wear, you want to change it out before you continue to hunt with it. Compound bowstrings are under a lot of strain constantly, and it is not something you want to have snap in your face. Take care of your bow, and it will take care of you.

For a recent Christmas, my lovely wife was kind enough to buy me a hard carrying case for my compound bow. Hard cases are handy just like a gun case is handy. It protects the bow and allows you to carry arrows and other equipment safely. I never liked just tossing my bow into my truck, along with all of my other gear while I was packing up for elk; now, thanks to that gift, I don't have to worry about damaging my bow or other bow-hunting equipment. Carrying cases come in a variety of price ranges, so pick one that suits your budget and how you'll use it. For example, if you are headed to Africa on a hunt, you might want to get a more expensive case with a good lock on it. If you are hunting your buddy's cornfield down the road, it might not be that big of a concern to have a lock on the case.

Do some research online or the old-fashioned way in person. Soon you will be out in your yard slinging arrows on a nice summer evening and hearing that telltale *thwack* as you practice for the bear opener, or elk or deer. One thing is for sure as far as bow hunting goes—it has 100 percent made me a better hunter all the way around. I normally hunt from the ground. With a bow, it forces me to slow down, to pay extra attention to the wind, and to be aware of all of my surroundings. If you have never tried bow hunting, I highly recommend it! I really think it will help make you a better hunter, as well, even if you don't succeed right away in taking an animal.

TRADITIONAL BOWS

People who want the ultimate challenge will work their way to the traditional bow, otherwise known as a longbow. It's about as basic as it gets—a plain wooden bow with a string and some arrows. No pins, no peep sight, no cams. Some hunters even only use arrows they make themselves with stone heads like a famous hunter called Tred Barta did. When I think of traditional modern bow hunters, I think of him. He was fairly popular on cable television for some time using only arrows he made himself with stone tips. He did it the hard way—the Barta way, as he would say. I really enjoyed watching his shows at the time, as it was not about the kill or taking a 700-yard shot at an animal with a bunch of hooting and hollering. It was the experience of the hunt, regardless of if an animal was killed. It was about getting close to the animal; it was about being a hunter. I think if you Google some of his shows, you might find them as enjoyable as I did. He was struck with a nasty cancer that has left him paralyzed, but he still remains active in fishing and with his charities. I would encourage anyone reading this book to support him by sending prayers, well wishes, and, if at all possible, donations to his charities. In case you are wondering, I am not sponsored by him nor do I know him personally. I just found him to be a pretty cool hunter with a seemingly big heart, and that is something we can all support.

People who shoot traditional bows usually do so instinctively— meaning the hunter is not relying on sight pins to guide him or her or a range finder (although I am sure some use it). They are relying on instinct, judging how far the shot is, and estimating how far they must pull back, along with determining the angle of the bow necessary to make the shot. This requires a bit more practice than using a compound bow. How far the arrow goes depends on how far you pull back and your angle of aim. Generally, the hunter wants to be under thirty yards depending on the range you practice. It is simplistic, instinctual, and primal. I've had a calling to try it for some time now, and perhaps when I am done writing this book I will take it up more seriously. There is an intangible allure with traditional bow hunting. The simple fact is that the whole process is so, well, simple—that makes it what it is. The key to using a traditional bow is practice, practice, and more practice. Real-world practice. Shoot uphill and downhill. Try along the side of a hill, jog in place, and shoot winded. Make your practice as real as you can so out in the field you are prepared for such situations.

Traditional bow hunting is not all that expensive to get into. You can get a new bow for just over one hundred dollars or go as high as you like. The wonderful thing about traditional bow hunting is the simplicity of it and the fact that it will not cost you an arm and a leg to get into, unlike compound bow hunting, depending on how expensive your taste is. If you have never bow hunted and want to get into it, stepping into the world of traditional bows is a great way to start.

The key point to remember with any bow hunting, in particular traditional, is consistency. Your nocking point should remain consistent, as should the weight of your arrow and arrowhead. Variations of these factors could cause issues in trying to get accurate shots. It is similar to rifle shooting. You want your cheek to rest on the same spot every time you take a shot with your rifle, and you want that same type of consistency with instinctive shooting of a bow. Don't sit around the house dry firing your bow either. That can cause your bow to break or other damage.

Another key point with traditional bows compared to compounds is that you do not want to pull back and then take aim while holding at full draw. You can do this with compounds, but it is not recommended with traditional bows. You want to gently release the arrow as soon as you have reached your nock point. Remember to focus on your target when you draw back—aim small and miss small. You want a quick, smooth, relaxed release. Continue to work on shooting, drawing back, and finding your nock point repetitively, consistently, and methodically. You want to have the muscle memory to just do the action when the time comes. That way, when the time does come, you really don't even think about it. I have reached that method with my rifle; I don't even think about raising and finding my cheek rest. It has become second nature.

If you are brand new to hunting with a traditional bow, you might want to try to hunt an animal that is slightly more forgiving if you happen to wound it. For example, a deer. I am not condoning wounding an animal, but I am making the case that a wounded deer is slightly less dangerous than a wounded bear. You see my point? If you have to go after a wounded animal with a traditional bow, I would choose a deer over a bear any day of the week.

MODERN RIFLES

With this discussion of modern rifles, I feel as though I'm going to open Pandora's box. Everyone will have an opinion on the subject, some may match my thoughts, and some may be completely different, while others could care less about hunting bears with a rifle. My opinion on using modern rifles for bears is simple—use a gun you are comfortable with, that is legal, and has a large enough caliber and bullet weight to take down deer, and you should be fine. Bears are interesting animals to hunt since it is likely you will see a 150-pounder strolling around, perhaps a 220-pounder eating some backcountry fruit, or you might come upon a dinosaur of 350 to 550 pounds or more of pure black commanding presence. Side note: it is not too often you will come across a 350- to 400-pound black bear in the lower forty-eight. There are plenty big bears out there, but you will soon notice online that there are lots of "350-pound" bears, when in reality it is likely a 250- to 285-pound bruin at most. People constantly overestimate the weight or size of bears. But I digress. Of course, right after I wrote this, someone in Washington bagged a 561-pound black bear in a cornfield, which will likely be a record for our state. And during December 2015 alone, a 700-pound black bear was hit by an off-duty police officer just outside of Yakima, Washington. That pig was famous for gorging itself in all the apple orchards that surround the area and was known by the locals. It was an exception to the rule.

Now, the rifle you are carrying might be good enough for the 150-pound little fella, but it might be slightly under what you want for the 350-pound or larger bruiser. My theory is to make sure it is enough for both situations. And let's not forget *shot placement*. I personally carry a Tikka T3 in .300 WSM (Winchester short magnum) with a 165-grain bullet. With proper placement, I have no problem knocking bears down of various sizes. The gun is probably a bit much for a smaller bear, but I feel comfortable with it on bigger bears. Better to have too much rifle than not enough.

There are several important factors to consider when deciding what rifle to use for bears. Caliber is number one. I don't like using anything less than a .30-.30. When I use my Winchester lever-action .30-.30, I like to use a heavier bullet weight—170 grain or so. I recently got a .243 stainless, which I am looking forward to using, but I would prefer not to use it for bears. I have the Mule (my .300 WSM) that I am partial to for bears. I have killed a few deer with that same .300 and think it is a bit of overkill, and I will likely move my deer hunting to the .243 rifle. I can feel it, Pandora's box is slowly creeping open at this point. I can hear what some of you might be thinking, and you are more than likely right about whatever it is you would like to bring up as far as challenging my advice for rifles. Frankly, if it's legal and gets the job done, that's all you need.

No matter what rifle you choose (or handgun, for that matter), choose a quality ammo. When I first started using my .300 WSM, I was picking a cheaper ammo that I will not name here. I noticed that the bullet weight retention, once it impacted the animal, was basically not there. Meaning the bullet would shatter and explode, and the animal might not drop right away even with good shot placement. I therefore went to a more expensive brand, and with a quality bullet I have had no issues since. It shoots accurately, and the bullet weight retention has been maintained nicely.

I have a love for lever actions, I don't know why—it must be the cowboy in me. The .30-.30 I have for bears could be a bit bigger. I would really like to purchase a .45-.70 lever-action, which is a popular caliber for bears in the lever-action world. I would be more comfortable with a bigger caliber than the .30-.30, but again it can really come down to where you hit the bear.

Open sights on your rifle might be something you'll want to consider. I refer to my .30-.30 as my brush gun for this reason. If I have to go after a bear in the brush and I don't have a shotgun with me, I break out the Winchester. Having the ability to locate and dispatch your target at close range in brush is key when tracking bears. Consider this when you are shooting with a scoped rifle. How quickly can you engage your target before your target is on top of you?

Of course, open sights also limit your ability to make the long shots if that is what the terrain requires and what you are into, so you will need to think about that, as well. Most of my shots are well under 100 yards for bear, deer, elk, or even coyote. It is just the way it pans out for me even though most of my rifles have a scope. Figure out what will work best for your hunting terrain and go with it. If you have wide-open areas, you might want a scoped weapon as opposed to an open-sight rifle. Of course, if you want more of a challenge, maybe you want iron sights.

Consider your rifle's action, too. Bolt-action rifles are the most accurate action you can get. They have few moving parts compared to a lever action, pump, or even a semiauto. Snipers usually use bolt actions for this reason. Consistency is a big part of shooting no matter what you choose to shoot. Train yourself to be consistent when shooting, and you will find yourself consistently accurate.

You should also think about what the weather is like where you are going to be hunting bears. I would not want a wood-stock rifle if I'm going to be hunting in wet areas, such as Alaska. If that were the case, I would go with a synthetic stock. You should also question the finish on your rifle. You might want to consider getting a stainless finish or even a powder coating on your rifle's barrel if you are in a wet environment all the time, which would not be unheard of for bears. I have been fine using my blued rifle in Washington, but it does require care, especially if I am in the backcountry hunting deer or bear and it is raining a lot.

I have installed on my bear gun (my .300 WSM) a Harris bipod. I do not have a sling on that rifle. I prefer to have it at the ready. If I need to put it down to rest or use a predator call, I use the bipod so the rifle does not have to lay in the dirt. I have carried that rifle all over the place, and the bipod has never let me down. I have lost a few coyotes because I was unable to get a shot off due to a sling catching on my backpack. Shortly after those experiences, I quit using a sling. Even this year deer hunting, I was on my way out of my backcountry camp, almost to the trail, and, sure enough, a 5 × 3 mule deer was standing right behind me at thirty yards. I was able to swing up and pop that deer to make it a successful hunt. Having my entire camp on my back, I am not sure I would have been able to get a shot off quickly if my rifle was shouldered with a sling or packed away on my backpack.

I am not saying that slings *aren't* handy; they are just not for me when bear hunting. I want to be able to make quick shots, even just for safety's sake. My dad, a Marine who received the Rifle Expert medal in boot camp, always has a sling—so take it for what you will. Everyone hunts a little differently.

SHOTGUNS

The use of shotguns can be handy for hunting black bears. Bears love to hang in nasty, thick brush. Sometimes a bear's chosen habitat does not lend itself to scoped rifles. Sometimes it is better to carry a shotgun depending on the terrain you're in. If you choose to use a shotgun where you are hunting, keep in mind your maximum range is much shorter than that of your rifle. You also need to remember what type of load you are carrying in the shotgun. Are you using buckshot or a slug? I prefer slugs when hunting bears unless I have to head into some brush after a wounded bear; then I am more than happy with buckshot. Stick with solid slugs and stay away from hollow-point slugs. It is better to have a good solid round for bears.

Practice and get familiar with the weapon, its action, and its shooting capability, as well as its recoil. Spend time getting to know it. You also might want to consider a shotgun with a slightly shorter barrel than one you would take duck hunting. The shorter the barrel, the shorter the accurate range, but sometimes those longer barrels can get in the way when you are crawling through brush on your hands and knees.

PISTOLS

Like the other weapons discussed, pistols can take down bears as long as the caliber is sufficient and the shot placement is good. Find out the regulations for bear hunting in your state, and see if pistols are allowed. Most states do allow hunting with a pistol, but the barrel length, in general, has to be at least four inches. I personally would not hunt with a pistol of any caliber less than a .357, but again, that is my personal preference. I normally carry a .45 when I am hunting, but normally that is for protection, not for hunting. I would be comfortable using the .45 to hunt, however. Know the limitations of the pistol for accurate distance and knock-down power. Pistols have a much shorter effective range than deer rifles, so be sure to treat them that way. Head to the range and see how far out you can shoot effectively. On a personal level, I would try to be within thirty yards when using a handgun—preferably less.

You may wish to add a scope to your pistol depending on its capabilities and yours shooting it. Remember that your hunting environment will dictate what weapons are most effective for bears. Having a scope doesn't mean your weapon's effective range has been extended, either. Pistols have limited range, as I am sure you are well aware. Again, consistency and knowledge of your weapon and ballistics are very important. If you have questions about ballistics for any of your weapons, you can easily look them up online to find out how far they drop at different ranges, what the muzzle velocity is, and so on.

MUZZLELOADERS

As in any discussion pertaining to weapons or calibers, everyone is going to have their own opinions and thoughts on this matter. I will be honest here, I have never used a muzzleloader, or smokepole as they are called, to hunt bears. Not because I am against it; I just don't own one. That being said, I have looked up, spoken to other hunters, and learned plenty on the subject, and here is what I have come up with. Basically, if you are knocking down deer with a muzzleloader, you should have no issues with bears. The key is waiting for the bear's shoulder to be forward, exposing the vitals.

Reading on the subject, there are plenty of people in agreement who use .50 caliber rounds with a 300-grain or heavier bullet on bears. You need to remember the limited range of the black-powder rifle, as well as the limitation of the bullet design (round ball or sabot). A bear-hunting legend, Jim Shockey—you probably never heard of him (a little sarcasm there)—uses a black powder gun often when hunting the big blackies that roam Vancouver Island, just north of my location. I say—if muzzleloaders are good enough for Jim Shockey, they are good enough for other bear hunters.

Stick with a quality round, as well. Take the time to find a quality round for the muzzleloader you are using. Find out what shoots accurately in your weapon and how well the bullet retains its weight. Remember, with bears, their fat and hair can really plug up entrance and exit wounds, so it is important to make a large wound to get a good blood trail if you have to track it.

Here is a picture of a good blood trail. It is not too often with bears, unlike deer or elk, that you get a really good blood trail.

SHOT PLACEMENT

I belong to several hunting forums online. Specifically, I like to hang out and read the bear stories. I learn a lot and like to help people who are starting out bear hunting. One question that doesn't get brought up much, which should, is the proper placement of shots on bears.

Proper shot placement on black bears, especially for those who are new to bear hunting, is something that should be studied in detail. Black-bear anatomy is different than that of deer and elk, and their fur is generally longer. The longer fur can make the bear look different than what it actually is underneath. Fur can hide the actual contours of its body, which causes hunters to misjudge exactly where the shoulder may be. Shooting too far back on a bear, causing a gut shot, is not uncommon for beginners. Let's discuss.

When you are observing a bear or any big game animal, you usually want to wait until you can get a good broadside shot to ensure a double-lung pass through, ideally. Bears seem to be constantly on the move, so you have to teach yourself some patience and wait for a shot. The key to good shot placement on black bears is to wait until they are broadside. Once broadside, wait until the bear's front leg, which is closest to you, moves forward as they step.

Photo courtesy of Justin Haug.

The importance of patience when bear hunting is expressed in this single photo. Observe the bear to ensure it does not have cubs with it. Cubs are often small and lag behind the momma bear. Be a cautious and ethical hunter—wait for the right shot on the right bear.

This technique is very important. The bear's shoulder blade, along with the massive muscle structure that surrounds it when the front leg is back, covers some of a bear's vitals. If you wait until the leg is forward, the shoulder blade and muscle mass moves further forward onto the body to expose more of the bear's vitals. Try to aim for the bear's armpit or just above it. This is generally how you want to approach it if you are on the ground with a bear.

Bears still offer decent shots when quartering away slightly—just be aware of how much they are quartering. With the age of the Internet, you can really learn a lot on just about any subject. A gentlemen named Keith Warren has a YouTube video titled, "Proper Shot Placement On A Black Bear." He gives an excellent example, physically, of how the shoulder and shoulder muscle block the vitals of a bear. If you have the chance, give it a look for further instruction. While I can instruct via text in a book, an actual video provides a good amount of advice that still pictures may lack regardless of how skillfully written their explanation might be.

In this picture, you can see that you are often left with little blood to track. In actuality, this is still a pretty decent blood trail for a bear. It is not uncommon to only have a speckling of blood. Hone your tracking skills every chance you get.

There are two rules I have come to live by when shooting bears. First, try to break a shoulder (or if you are lucky enough, both shoulders) with your first shot; second is to keep firing until the bear is all the way down. Every single time I have let a bear get up, he has run off, and I either have to recover him in some thorny brush or go in after him to finish the job, neither of which are my favorite things to do. The idea behind the shoulder break is simple enough—it slows down the bear so if it is not finished with the first shot, you can fire off another shot quickly to do it.

When you are in a tree stand, shot placement is a different story. The angle at which you are above the bear can make a major difference in how and where that arrow or bullet penetrates the body cavity of the bear. The angle at which you shoot a bear is extremely important when bow hunting from a stand. You do not want an angle that's too steep, as it could cause the arrow to glance or miss the vitals. The less of an angle you allow, the better. This is something you need to keep in mind, especially when setting up your bait station, but we'll touch on that in the baiting chapter. Try to picture an imaginary line where your shot will go through the bear before you shoot. It may help if you pause then take a shot.

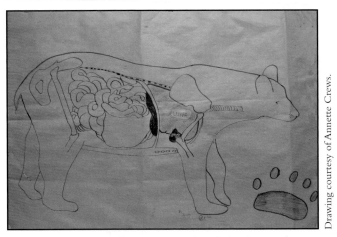

In this picture, you can see the vitals of the bear and, more importantly, the non-vital areas.

You must avoid shooting too far back on the bear's body to avoid a paunch shot. Stomach shots make for a painful death and a big-time pain in tracking the animal. Really take your time and study up on bear shot placement, as it will save you frustration in the future if you get the chance to seal the deal on a bear. If you find vegetable or other food-like matter or fecal matter where your animal was standing when it was hit, you likely hit too far back. Be fully prepared both mentally and physically to put in the time and effort to find that bear. The animal deserves it. If you can rest your rifle on your pack, steady it on a tree, or so on to ensure a steady shot, you should do it. If you are archery hunting, breathe, calm yourself, and aim small, as I mentioned earlier. Hopefully, you have practiced enough in the off season so shooting is not much more than muscle memory. Waiting for the bear's closest shoulder to you to move forward is key. Wait for it, then release or squeeze that trigger.

Photo courtesy of Justin Haug.

In this picture, notice how the black bear is quartering slightly toward the camera and has the closest front shoulder pushed back. Wait for the bear to completely show broadside and, just as important, wait for that shoulder to be moved forward, exposing the vitals.

If you make a poor shot, it is not uncommon for the bear to head into thick cover to try to avoid detection. They will bury themselves under logs, in holes, climb trees, and do just about anything else to avoid you. But if you go in after them, they are fair game. Like any cornered, wounded animal, the bear can and will attack, so you have to be prepared. Always be

Photo courtesy of Justin Haug.

Here, the bear is broadside, which is not a terrible shot by any means. My only concern is that the shoulder is not forward, and the brush is slightly in the way. Depending on what you are using for a weapon, this could be a no go shot situation, especially with a bow. It is better to pass than to wound the bear with a poor shot.

mentally ready to go in after a bear if you must. Going into brush after any wounded animal, especially a bear, requires a great amount of caution because they can hide so well, and they can do some real damage to you very quickly. A few times, I have searched for a bear that someone in my family or even I shot, and if the bear had not been found dead, it would have been on top of me before I would have had much chance to react.

Getting on your hands and knees crawling through brush is common when looking for a wounded bear. Do not solely rely on blood trails when you are searching. I have smelled a bear before I have seen it a few times, and so have my hunting buddies. Make sure to be meticulous in your search by looking not only for blood but also for tracks, leaves that have been overturned, snapped twigs, and blood under leaves, stumps, branches, and grass. Look for blood at the bear's height on any brush or trees it might have brushed against. If you lose the trail, step back to the last marked location and do circles around the area that get wider and wider as you go. This is all basic knowledge if you already hunt big game, but for those of you who are jumping right into bear hunting, tracking is a fine art that can take some practice. Volunteer to track anytime you can, as it is always a great learning experience.

Hidden in this picture is my brother's bear that I was tracking for several dozen yards through a wall of brush on my hands and knees. This picture was taken before the brush was cleared; notice in this picture it just appears to be brush. In reality, I could smell the bear a dozen or so yards away.

After the brush was cleared, you could see how easy it would have been to miss that bear if we were not paying close attention. This is a fine example of how the bear could have attacked me if it were not already dead. Be extremely cautious when tracking your bear.

If you are successful and retrieve the bear, you have, of course, accomplished something great. A bear is a wonderful animal to be treasured and enjoyed by the whole family. Take a minute to learn a little bit about that particular bear before starting to process it. I always enjoy learning as much as I can about the bears I take. I really let my mind wander, too, with deer

MOULTRIE   ○   59°F   MOULTRIECAM   17 MAY 2015 10:40 pm

Photo by Fred Moyer.

As soon as this color-phase bear moves that leg closest to you (the front right leg) forward, shoot! It looks as if it is getting ready to move as we speak. It wouldn't be a bad shot as the bear stands currently, either.

or elk, even coyote, about their life story. Where did this bear get that scar on its nose, why is this antler deformed, and so on. I always like to check the teeth of my bear (to help figure out the age), and always check the stomach contents once the bear has been gutted.

You can tell quite a bit from a bear's teeth, and each bear has its own story to tell. I've found bears that are completely missing their front teeth, some bears have cleaner teeth that seem undamaged, and some just have some minor discoloration or major depending on their general diet. You see, basically, the worse the teeth are, the older the bear likely is. A bear's teeth usually will not start to show

In this photo, I was checking the teeth of the bear I shot while in Alaska. I always check the teeth of the bear for an initial estimate of its age.

much wear and tear until about five years old. The aging starts off with discoloration, then you'll see wearing of the teeth, and finally major decay.

You can see that these teeth are generally in good shape; it turns out this was a three-year-old bear.

Photo by Justin Haug.

In this picture, you can see specific wear and tear on the lower jaw teeth, not to mention yellowing of the teeth and flat-tipped canines. All these are signs of an older bear.

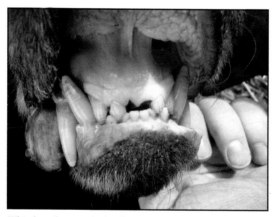

This bear has cracked yellow teeth and is missing his two front teeth. I guess we know what he should have asked about for Christmas! This is an older bear.

Like I said, don't forget to check your bear's stomach contents once you are ready to go out of the area. The contents may surprise you. Most importantly, the contents will tell you what the bear has been eating in the area, so you can now target that food source if you can find it.

The real key points of shot placement and tracking bears are fairly simple. Number one, wait until that broadside shot presents itself and the bear has its shoulder closest to you moved forward. Number two, aim small and slightly lower than where you would on a deer. If you prefer, you can always break that shoulder, but you will find waiting for a good shot

With the bear's stomach split open, it is easy to see that this bear was eating mainly vegetable matter. In fact, this was a spring bear that was eating green grass and, more to the point, was stripping trees of their bark to eat the cambium layer. That is the white you see in the stomach material. It was stripping a tree when I shot it.

You can see a big difference between a spring bear's stomach and one of a bear that was killed in the late summer or early fall. This is the stomach of a bear that charged me but was in the midst of a blackberry patch moments before I shot. Several times I have split open a bear's stomach in summer and found tons of berries—always smelling like berry pie.

of those vitals will help anchor that bear. Number three, which is different for everyone, keep firing at the bear until it is down. Finally, number four, be prepared to go into nasty brush and expect to have little trail to follow. Bears will make you work for them, that's for sure. Check every nook and cranny, under logs, in stumps, under brush, and everywhere because once hit, they love to hide. Good things come to those who work for it, though! Find that bear!

Chapter Three

Baiting Bears

Before we get into the meat and potatoes (no pun intended) of baiting, I would like to take a minute to discuss the politics that surround baiting. Baiting bears has been under attack by antihunting advocates for several years now with some limited success, I am sad to say. Not to mention, there are some hunters who do not like the idea of baiting in general, whether it be for bears or deer and the like. When I say antihunters, I am not referring to those who just don't agree with hunting. I have no problem with people who have other opinions than mine; they are free to be wrong if they want. I am referring to those who spew forth nothing less than their hate speech to hunters, threaten us with violence, or wish harm upon us. For them, I have little patience.

We, as hunters, must collectively stand firm and together to oppose the anti's agendas. Whether or not you bait for bears does not matter. If you hunt or fish, the issue of baiting matters to you and your children directly. Typical whack job antihunting political strategy is as follows: divide your opponents (pit hunters who bait against those who don't), energize your political base supporters (do-nothing yuppies who have more money than common sense), and conquer. Today it is baiting (Maine and Michigan bear hunters, you know what I am talking about), and tomorrow it is hunting altogether. Do not be fooled, they want to end all hunting and trapping regardless of method. I am personally determined not to let that happen. California trappers just lost their right to trap bobcats. Was it due to a low population of bobs? Nope, it was because some loud-mouthed anti made enough noise and raised enough of a stink that it became outlawed with no science to back it, in my opinion. Stand together or fall apart.

Do not think that they want to stop baiting because it is lazy or unsporting, according to some of their arguments on the subject. Some archery hunters might find rifle hunting unsporting, so they use a bow. My point is, the attack on baiting is an attack on hunting. Period. So, take a stand for hunting and defend baiting whenever possible because it is ultimately an attack on your way of life as a hunter. We hunters and fishers had better learn to unite, or we are going to fall in this political fight. I encourage all of you reading this book to join a political hunting group of your choice that you feel best represents your views and donate time, effort, and money. Personally, I am a life member of the National Rifle Association, a member of the Mule Deer Foundation (MDF}, the Rocky Mountain Elk Foundation, and SCI, which are all great organizations to belong to. I would also like to give a shout out to the Michigan Bear Hunters Association, www.mibearhunters.org, an organization we should all consider joining even if we don't live in Michigan. The work they do to promote and maintain bear hunting deserves our support.

As many of you see in the media, card-carrying animal-rights advocates constantly try to demonize hunting and hunters in any way possible by trying to bring down our image to those who may not hunt. Ever seen the movies *Open Season*, *Wolverine*, and so on? I encourage and challenge all of you to raise your voice and no longer be a silent majority but face off and challenge antihunting wherever you may see it—in the newspapers, online, on Facebook, wherever the ignorance of antihunting rears its ugly head. Not in a crude, vulgar fashion but rather with facts, family tradition, and general common sense. Learn how to express and defend our heritage. Get educated on the subject so you can properly defend our stance on hunting, and pass along that defense to your children, who likely face similar antihunting in public education.

Our image matters, so when you are hunting and you come across hikers, nonhunters, and others, take the time to say hello and to present yourself as who you are—maybe a father and son spending quality time together or a veteran enjoying your favorite pastime. Perhaps you are like me, at times, a solo hunter getting back to nature and feeling more at home in the woods than in any church or populated metropolis. Maybe you are a daughter getting away with your dear old dad for the weekend. It is about the friends and family as much as the pursuit of the animal, if not more.

That being said, let us discuss some benefits of baiting bears. First and foremost, to me, the number one benefit in baiting is that hunters can usually ensure they are not taking a sow with cubs, as they have ample time to observe the bear before shooting. Female black bears do not reach sexual maturity until they are four or five years old, and the males mature around the five- or six-year mark (according to blueplanetbiomes.org). Therefore, it is important for the continued proliferation of black bears that we as hunters try to take mature males.

Second, bear baiters can take mature boars that have had their chance to pass along their genes while passing on younger boars and, more importantly, younger sows who have yet to reach sexual maturity. Bear baiters have the ability to sit and observe the animal to learn from bear body language and how they react to one another. It is a great opportunity for those who get to do it. This also allows younger hunters to observe all sorts of animals that may come to the bait station, which increases their love of watching all sorts of game. Really being able to take the time to see if the bear has a blocky head and broad shoulders, like a boar should, or if the rump is big with a smaller, narrow head, like a sow, is a great advantage.

Those who have baited know how much work and patience go into setting up a bait station, as well as maintaining a bait site, and then tearing down and doing a proper cleanup. It is not simply throwing food out for a bear to come to. There are strict regulations as to what can be fed to bears, appropriate signage for bait sites, as well as other specific dos and don'ts at baiting sites.

There are many things to consider when looking for good bait sites. Ideally, you want to find areas of bear traffic, so look for bear scat, bear tree damage, creek bottoms, bear prints, and the like. Water sources are key to bears, so if you have the option to set up by a water source, do it! Don't be afraid to take time to locate some good game trails for bears. Use Google Earth to help locate corridors that bears may take, funnel areas at the bottoms of canyons and ridgetops, and other natural paths on which bears travel. Proper prior scouting for bear sign can help take out some of the work required when setting up a bait station.

Once you have an area picked out, you need to set up your bait barrel. Your first priority should be to find a strong, healthy tree that you can chain or cable the bait barrel to, which will stop the bear from dragging or rolling the fifty-five-gallon barrel away from the site. You can usually pick up barrels online for 60 to 130 dollars. Make sure they did not previously house hazardous materials or other materials that may make the bear sick. You want to have a good clean barrel. Keep an eye out online and post on your local Craigslist if you are having trouble finding one. A good tip I once read in *Bear Hunting Magazine* was to get a light-colored bait barrel. The idea is the light-colored barrel helps draw in light during low-light situations to allow for a better silhouette of the bear in morning or dusk hours. It is a simple idea but one that is easy to miss!

Next you will want a strong chain or cable to secure the barrel to a tree. Make sure you have enough chain or cable to go around the tree and through the barrel, as you don't want to get all the way out to the bait site and not be able to secure the barrel. You will want to try to place the barrel near cover for the bear to make the bear feel secure. Cover means safety, and this will give the bear a false sense of security. However, make sure that the bait barrel is also visible from your tree stand or ground blind depending on how you want to hunt.

Here is a great example of why you'd better secure your bait barrel to a tree using a chain or cable. That is a pig of a bear! If a bear makes your fifty-five-gallon drum look that small, SHOOT!

You may want to set up the bait barrel and hop in your stand to judge how the barrel looks relative to your position. It is not uncommon to place a few logs on top of the bait barrel to help secure the bait so raccoons and other nontarget animals can't access it easily. Logs about four or five inches around should be fine. Try to funnel the bears, or force them with logs or other means, to face broadside while they eat, which will allow for a good clean kill shot. The last thing you want is for bears to come in and not expose their broadside or have them be blocked by brush or other objects you did not foresee. Don't be afraid to set a log or other object down on the ground to provide an idea of the size of the bear. Use a log that is five and half to six feet long. If you cannot find a log, you can use some marker tape and have them on sticks at that distance. Anything to let you know the length of the bear. Any bear close to the length of the log (or the marker tape) will be a decent black bear. Planning your bait site carefully will pay off in the end.

You will want to create your ground blind or secure your tree stand as early as legally possible. This way the bears traveling the area get used to seeing that new item in the woods. Hopefully, they do not notice your tree stand, but they could easily notice the ladder leading up to it. I have used a ladderless, or climbing, tree stand for hunting. While it is nice to have when baiting, I would really recommend either a permanently built tree stand or one with a ladder. The climbing-style tree stands, in my opinion, seem a bit awkward to use when compared to a ladder-style tree stand. They are noisy to bring out to the location, cumbersome, and a hassle to get up and down the tree. Make sure when you are in the tree stand you are not silhouetted and have several branches to help break up any movements you might make while in the stand. You will want your tree stand to be twenty to thirty yards from your bait barrel. This allows you to be in good shot range while not being close enough to make bears reluctant or nervous—a key point. Safety needs to come first, so make sure to pick a tree that does not have any rot on it (or signs of bug infestation) but is strong and healthy. Woodpecker holes in a tree are a sign to stay away from using it. Keep in mind, the higher you go in the tree, the smaller the vital area of the bear will be. If you are going to be hunting from a tree stand, take time to practice shooting from one in the off season.

It will not be uncommon to get a mother and cub coming into a bait site. Be patient and watch to make sure you are not taking a sow with cubs.

If you are hunting from a tree stand, make sure to tie off as soon as you get up in the stand—meaning use a fall-arrest system. It is vitally important for you and your family that you immediately tie off when in the stand. Falling is a major hunting injury every year that can easily be prevented. Get familiar with your fall-arrest system, or harness, before you head out into the woods. Follow the instructions to the letter when using your harness. You do not want the leg straps to be super tight when donning the harness, but you want them snug. I work construction, generally, and it is known that a fall from a small vertical distance can kill someone, even a distance of four feet.

Think about what you are tying off to—your life depends on it. Basically, whatever you secure your fall-arrest lanyard to should be able to hold the weight of a car. If you don't think it can hold a vehicle, don't tie off to it. This is a good rule of thumb to follow. I say this amount of weight not because I think you might be a heavy person but because when you fall, you generate about that much force even within a short distance. Granted, your options may be limited in the wild, but—trust me—it is better to be safe than sorry. You do not want to be one of the hunters who gets paralyzed or worse because you didn't want to tie off or tied off incorrectly. Falling happens extremely quickly, and it only takes a fraction of a second to do irreparable damage. Also, if at all possible, you want to tie off above your head. That way if you fall, you fall that much less before the fall is arrested—or maybe your lanyard is already almost tight, so you do not fall at all. Finally, know that being in a harness while suspended can take its toll on your body within minutes, as it cuts off blood to your legs. Have a predetermined way of getting back on the stand or getting help if you happen to fall. You do not want to be hanging in a harness overnight.

I almost forgot to mention—take a good look at your harness every day before you put it on. Are there any cuts or tears in the harness itself or in the lanyard? Are the connections in good shape? Has it been exposed to any sort of chemical that could cause it to cake or corrode? How does the lanyard hook look? Does it work properly? Store your harness per the manufacturer's recommendations, which in general means hang it in a cool dry place out of direct sunlight. Don't just throw it on the floor of your garage, where it can come into contact with oil, chemicals, or other damaging substances. When it gets wet, hang it to dry. If there are any burns, tears, frays, or other damage, you should replace it. It is not worth risking your life over. Always fully read and understand the manufacturer's recommendations on both the tree stand setup requirements and the safety harness before using them.

Your ground blind should be equally, if not more, camouflaged as the surrounding terrain and at a safe distance from the bear site. If you are using a commercial-brand blind, you might want to consider placing some local brush around it to help blend in the edges. Bears will be coming from all around, so try to position the blind in an area where you can make an ethical shot, you have a good view of the bait barrel, and the bears are not likely to come into it. If you are using a rifle, you can obviously set it farther away from the site than if you are using a bow. I always clear the ground of any debris, sticks, leaves, and so on that might make noise if I step on them. I do this elk hunting all the time by clearing it away so bare dirt is all I'm stepping on. It would be a shame if you took all this time to set up the site, waited for a good bear to show up, and then had to reposition or move for whatever reason only to snap a twig and have the bear bug out because of the noise. Proper planning of your site and blind or stand can make all the difference. Take your time to consider these challenges as you do your setup. I also grab some local sappy tree branches and rub them on my clothing, under my arms, and on my pants as a natural cover scent.

I also want to point out that if you are going on an outfitted bait hunt, you should listen to your outfitter's advice. Do not be afraid to ask questions on what to expect, how far the stand is from the site (for shooting purposes), how bad the bugs are, and consider if you are scared of heights because even something as simple as that can make a difference. Do not forget a rope to raise or lower your weapon down to the ground—and have it unloaded when you do so for safety. Do not hold items in your hands when climbing the tree stand ladder. This is good way to end up on the ground.

Here we have a nice-looking color-phase bear broadside. What more could a bear hunter ask?

On the topic of early setup of blinds or stands, I can relate a story. I was deer hunting this past season. I had hiked out to my favorite camping spot, which is a funnel at the top of a canyon with lots of game trails right through where I camp. My tent is small, a single-man tent that is the same color as the surrounding grass at that time of year, kind of an off-yellow. Really, when set up, it almost looks like a boulder. I was sitting next to my tent near dusk the night before the deer opener. Several deer were walking through the burned-out woods along the edge of the small clearing I was camped in. Every single one of them stopped and looked at this very new item in the field. They didn't smell it—the wind was wrong—but they visually noticed it. The tent was tied down and tight, not moving. They knew that this object was not there earlier. Their memory of the place told them something wasn't right. It is the same with bears—the earlier you can get your stands or blinds set up, the more accustomed to the item the animal will be, the more comfortable the animal will be, and the more successful you as a hunter will be.

Another key point to keep in mind is the prevailing wind in the area. If you are going to be hunting the bait site in the late afternoon until dusk, the prevailing wind will likely be different than if you were hunting the site first thing in the morning due to the thermals in the area. Give yourself a path to get to the site and stick to it. If you need to clear some brush or branches, do so before the season or right at the start. Once you get the bait barrel in a position you can shoot satisfactorily from at your blind or stand, you are ready to put in the bait.

Obey all laws regarding the type of bait you use. Chocolate is illegal for baiting in several states, for example. If you check around, you will find most hunters have a favorite bait they like to use, such as doughnuts, old pastries, old fish, roadkill (where legal), all the way to popcorn. The key with bear bait is that you want it to smell. Bears have extremely powerful noses, so if you can get the smell of the bait out, it can help attract bears to your site. Do not simply place the bait inside the barrel. You will want to spread the bait throughout the bait site, on top of the bait barrel, and so forth. The idea is to make the bear work for the bait while keeping it interested and coming back for more.

Do not forget to set up a trail camera or two in the area, so you can see what is coming into your bait site. Checking trail cameras is a lot like Christmas morning for me—it is always so fun to see what you may have recorded on the camera. Have the camera(s) face the bait barrel, without directly facing the sun, as that can wash out the picture. Next, step in front of the camera by the bait barrel to use yourself as a reference for size. The bait barrel will help in this regard, too, but it is nice to have a person as a reference point for size. If you are lucky enough to have more than one camera, place one on any incoming trails that you think the bears may travel. Do not forget to secure the camera to the tree, and you may want to use gloves while installing cameras, so you don't get food smell (or human scent) on the camera. A commercial-grade bear box is also recommended. I have had more than one camera get attacked by bears, and they were not even at bait sites! Also, do not get fooled when looking at bears in relation to your barrel on the trail cam. Pay special attention to where the bear is in relation to the barrel itself. If the bear is a bit far away from the barrel or closer to the camera, it may appear bigger than it actually is. Take your time when you check out the photos. Also, don't forget to turn it on—not that I would ever have done something like that. Fresh batteries are always helpful, too.

This photo is from a trail camera—which is always there on the trail even when you're not. A trail camera is invaluable when working a bait site. It can tell you all sorts of information about the time of day, temperature, and, more importantly, the size of bears coming into your site!

Pay special attention to the time of day a bear is hitting your bait. A bear will frequently be consistent about when it decides to come in for a snack. This can help you plan your hunt, as well, so you are not stuck in the stand all day if your time is limited. If a bear on all fours comes in, on camera or in person, that is as tall as the barrel is when the barrel is vertical, you have yourself a good-sized bear, and you might want to take a good look at it.

If the shoulder is close to the top of the barrel or above, it's a good-sized bear. Experienced baiters use the barrel as a size reference for bears.

You will find that some hunters use scent rags hung in trees around the bait site. This helps spread the chosen scent out of the area, which can bring in bears from the surrounding area. This can help get bears into your site, which is your number one goal. You can also place a solid scent block in a breathable game bag hung in a tree nearby to help draw in bears. Or, you can drip grease or other foods on game trails that lead to or are near the site. If you pour some grease or other liquid attractant in the area around the bait barrel, this will cause the bear to step into the grease puddle, which will get it on its feet. From there, it will travel along and help to spread the scent of the food from the bait site. This will in turn attract other bears, which smell the attractant on the ground, to the bait site.

One of the fun parts about baiting is finding what works and using different recipes and techniques. Experiment with different options and find what works best in your area. Another way to initially get bears to your site is to set up the site on a ridgetop if there is bear sign there. From that location, you can then try a honey burn or bear bomb during morning or late afternoon. The idea of a honey burn is simple: grab your camp stove or jet boiler, and scorch honey or other sugary material, such as Jell-O, in a frying pan, maybe add some bacon, and start creating smoke. You are trying to burn it and create smoke to carry the scent down off the ridgeline (or your general area) and hopefully down into valleys on either side of the ridge. As the smoke builds and floats down, it will permeate throughout the lower area to attract bears to the site of the burn. Simple, effective, plus you get to eat some honey-soaked bacon after you're done. Who wouldn't like this technique!?

Bear bombs are commercially available bait-scent bombs that you can buy for a small price—around ten bucks or so. Think of a flea bomb—only for bears, it's not made to kill them but to attract. Again, make sure you check your local game regulations. They sell these bear bombs here in Washington, but they are illegal to use, so really check over your game regs. If you have a question, contact a warden and get it in writing in case it ever comes up. These bombs come in a variety of scents, such as bacon, cake frosting, anise oil, sow in heat, and so on. Do not use it as a deodorant. You might not like the results. The bear bomb can be used as a substitute for, or in addition to, your honey burn.

Be sure to make a hole in the bait barrel so the bears can get to the bait, obviously. I don't remember what hunting show I was watching, but years ago on the Sportsman's Channel, I saw an outfitter use popcorn as bait. He liked it as bait, as it was light (you could bring garbage bags of it out and not strain) and it was easy to distribute to the bears. They simply cut small holes at the bottom of the barrel to allow the popped corn to roll out as it was eaten. Bears couldn't eat huge amounts of the popcorn, and it kept the bears interested enough to stick around and eat it. It also didn't fill up the bears for long, which made the bears hit the bait station more frequently. Plus, it's cheap!

You also want to keep the bait dry in the barrel, so try to keep out rain by having a good, secure top. If water happens to get in and the bait sits for a while, it could start to get moldy, which you don't want. Regardless of your bait, you also want the hole to be near the bottom of the barrel; this way, it is less likely to allow water into the barrel, which causes the spoilage I mention. Also, the bear is forced to eat the older bait at the bottom first, as the fresh bait will be at the top, which reduces the chance of spoilage.

You do not have to spend a ton of money on bait. You can often go to bakeries to get old items, such as pastries and the like, for next to nothing. Be sure to check these before you go out and buy a bunch of items. How you physically get the bait to the site is another matter. If you're in a remote site, are you going to use your four wheeler, backpack it in, have horses take it, pack goats—what? These are things to consider. Plus, adding raw ingredients to bait you already have, for example bags of plain old granulated sugar, can have amazing effects on your bait. If you have a Costco membership, you can even get granulated sugar or brown sugar, whatever you like, by the pallet if you are so inclined. However, I want to stress, you really need to check your state's hunting regulations before you select bait to use.

When you replenish your bait site, try to use the same routine as often as possible. Bears will often hang out by a food source, and a bait site is just that. To a bear's mind, it is a food source until it is all gone. If you do the same thing over and over, the bear will become used to it and not think of you as a threat. In addition, it will help limit your scent to specific areas that you use over and over. Apply a scent mix as you go to and from the bait site. Using a standard spray bottle, spray the area as you go. This will help cover your scent and add further scent with the hope it gets picked up by bears, which will then hit your bait. If you are having trouble getting bears to the bait, you may need to add a bait topper to it, such as Bear Crack or other similar products. There are all sorts of different kinds of scents and flavors from which to choose. Trial and error—find out what they like in your specific area.

The fury of a large hungry black bear is not something to mess with.

Here is the result of bear damage—what a bear can do. It never hurts to reinforce your bait stations. Try to bend that steel on your own, and see how far you get! Pure power!

You can see how important scent is when baiting bears. You really need to work on casting scent out as much as possible and have it lead back to your site to keep and hold bears. Along with scent, bugs can be a major factor when baiting because lots of baiting in certain states happens during the springtime. If you are baiting in the spring, Thermacell is a wonderful addition to any bear hunt. It quietly burns off a scent that mosquitos hate and can be invaluable to keep the madness of bites from overtaking you. Remaining still on the tree stand or blind is essential, and bug control can really help with this. You will read on the package that you're not supposed to use Thermacell in the rain; however, that has not stopped me from doing so. I have also drenched my hats and coats in DEET bug repellant, which works wonders. A day or so before your hunt, if you spray down your clothes and hat with DEET, and let it dry into the fabric, you are already on the way to fighting off those flying bloodsuckers. If you are headed to

Alaska or British Columbia, you will no doubt need a mosquito net to place over your hat or to buy one that comes with a hat. It's cheap, effective, and worth every penny even if you don't use it.

Once the bears start to hit your bait, they will eat until the bait is gone, then they will take off. You obviously want to avoid this from happening. Be prepared to spend time and effort restocking your bait site often. You need to check your bait site(s) to figure out how often they are getting hit and how much bait you need to add. You do not want to lose bears because they come to your site but leave since you did not rebait.

Baiting takes a lot of work, but the payoff of getting to simply spend time with the bears while they are eating and being able to be selective on a nice mature boar is a wonderful reward for a job well done.

Let's not forget a very important part of baiting—the end of season cleanup. Whatever you bring in, you should bring out. Bait sites are unsightly, in my opinion, if left out. In addition, not properly cleaning up the area could lead to a littering fine. It is our responsibility as baiters to clean up after ourselves and leave the woods just as we found them. So, take care of any mess you make. Pack it in, pack it out.

I wanted to dig deep to find my readers some true quality bits of information that will help them in baiting for bear. Who popped into my head but a guy I have spoken with a few times in the past. Dale Denney from Bearpaw Outfitters is a well-respected outfitter in the hunting community in North America with an A+ rating from the Better Business Bureau. With outfitting businesses in Idaho, Utah, Washington, and Montana, as well as being the owner of Hunting-Washington.com and having made numerous TV appearances, it is safe to say he has plenty of experience in bear hunting and baiting. Dale has been bear hunting since he could follow behind his dad. He has thirty-eight years of professional outfitting experience to be exact. I had the privilege to pick his brain for bear baiting gold nuggets, as I like to call them, and the following are the results. A little side note here, I am not endorsed by Bearpaw Outfitters in any way. This is information that I wanted to pass along because I found it relevant and useful. I hope you enjoy!

Question: When you initially start a bait site, do you use a honey burn or other scent attractor to get the bears coming into the bait? If so, are there any secrets you'd like to share?

Answer: *I like any strong attractive scent for bears that is easy to place and will travel great distances. Anise, fish, meat, sweets, and the like. You can bury a* *quart jar full of fish scraps for a few months, when you dig it up it will be liquid that is very strong. Dip a stick in that and leave it at your bait.*

Question: For your bait, what is your normal go-to recipe?

Answer: *Whatever I can get lots of, bears eat a lot! I've used butcher meat scraps, bakery goods, old bread, grains, popcorn, restaurant scraps, and even dog food. One thing I've noticed, different bears like different things best. I've watched different bears eat different things from the same bait, so it doesn't hurt to provide some diversity. Remember, if you bait in remote country the bears aren't as picky as bears that have a choice of baits put out by many different baiters!*

Question: What do you use to secure the bait containers?

Answer: *Chain or cable a barrel to a stump.*

Question: What do you look for in a good bait site?

Answer: *I like remote locations in good bear country away from most human activity and with water within a reasonable distance. You don't want your bear crossing roads or having to travel for water.*

Question: Any nuggets of advice for the beginning bear baiter?

Answer: *Place your bait in a position where hopefully the bear turns quartering away from you to feed. From the beginning, leave lots of human scent to condition your bears to get used to human scent, then you don't have to worry about it. Put your stand back away so you aren't right on top of the bait, as bears are sensitive to any little noises. The farther away you are, the better. When you bait the station, bang your bait bucket on the side of the bait barrel so the bears know you were there, and do this consistently (this acts like a dinner bell). When you go in to hunt, bang the bucket, get in your stand, and be quiet. Always use unscented shampoo, laundry soaps, and fabric softener when hunting.*

Question: What is a common mistake in baiting that beginners should avoid?

Answer: *Don't bait in close proximity to human residences, campgrounds, or near other baiters or popular hunting areas where other baiters are likely baiting. Get away from the road! Get remote!*

So there you have it, guys and gals. While simplistic, there are some dos and don'ts when baiting. I hope if you are just starting to bait, this chapter will have given you a good base of knowledge to build off of. If you are an old-timer bear baiter, well, I hope you at least learned a little something new. Best of luck to you on bear baiting! I am sure you'll love it.

Chapter Four

Spotting and Stalking

———

I have heard from some people that it is not possible to spot and stalk bears in thick brush. There have been a few people who have come to me with this opinion. Or they will claim that their state has thicker brush than where I hunt in Washington and so on. But I can say without hesitation that this simply isn't true. Most of these people were either hound hunters or bear baiters, both of whom I respect completely and support 100 percent wholeheartedly. It is true, however, that spotting and stalking black bears will never get you as many bears as running hounds or baiting will. We humans just cannot compete with a group of dogs when it comes to having a heightened sense of smell. But what I can promise you is if you put in the time, focus, learn bear behavior, learn the terrain you are hunting in, and get a little luck and wind on your side, you can almost touch a bear on the ground without even using a blind. Spotting and stalking is 100 percent possible even in nasty brush, you just need to pick your situation so you can capitalize on it. Manipulating your surroundings to benefit your hunting success percentage is often what you need to do.

Believe it or not, I have been within three steps of a bear while on the ground (and if I hadn't backed up, I would have been within touching distance) with no blind, and I was in the wide open. It was an extremely close and tense situation for me (and the bear once he figured it out). I have also been so close to a deer that the whiskers on her nose tickled my cheek as she came in to smell me. This was all because I am a hunter by nature, deep in my heart of hearts, and because I was able to be in the right place at the right time and briefly fool the animals. Of course, that doesn't mean spotting and stalking is an easy task, even on open, easy walking terrain. It takes discipline, patience, the right wind, the right situation, and the willingness to pass on a shot or to accept blowing a stalk. Hunting bears is all about food sources, wind direction, and the right strategy for the current situation.

To start out, if you are going to spot and stalk, you need some decent optics. Don't use the scope of your gun to glass hillsides. We all know how unsafe that is, and it breaks the first rule of hunter education: don't point your gun at something you do not intend to shoot. If you are just starting out but don't want to break the bank, buy yourself the best pair of binoculars you can afford. That way you can use them for general hunting, and you don't have to spend a grand or more on a spotting scope. I prefer Leupold optics. That is, of course, my personal preference; I am not sponsored by them, either. I am sure my father or brother would tout the joys of Vortex or Swarovski, but I am a Leupold guy. I love their lifetime warranty, and from what I have experienced, their customer service is excellent. I am a gold-ring guy for life.

Photo by Justin Haug.

The absolute glory and majesty of nature cannot be expressed through words, actions, or even thought. It can only be experienced. Here I am on a dream come true Alaskan black-bear hunt, spot-and-stalk style—the only way to go!

Predators, in my experience, like edges of terrain, tree-line edges, fence edges, brush edges, and the like. I don't know why, I just know they do. I usually focus on glassing edges like this; or, if the terrain allows, any openings that look like they might contain bear. Once you get to know what to look for with bear, you will often think, "Hey, that place looks like it will be a good spot for a bear," and if you hold steady and have a little patience, a bear just might show itself. Get up high and position yourself so you are able to glass down onto an area, provided the wind allows you to do so. Wind is a paramount factor for finding bears. You can fool their eyes and ears, but you aren't fooling their nose. Remember that—you will never fool their nose. Edges of woods are great because they allow sunlight to hit brush, perhaps allowing for berries to grow, yet still allow a bear quick access to cover and safety. I have hunted many tree lines with walls (yes, literally walls) of blackberries that grew along the edges only to find a bear standing up and eating contently away on the luscious berries.

Here is a good example of a color-phase bear. While still a black bear, its fur is not technically black. Black bears come in all sorts of colors, including chocolate, blonde, red, and even sometimes white, known as a sunbear.

You will often hear bears before you see them depending on where you hunt. This is an important point, remember it. A comfortable bear will make noise and snort, tear into stumps, and thrash brush seemingly without a care in the world. If you listen carefully as you walk tree lines or mountain ridges, creek bottoms or farmers' fields, your hearing could be your first line of offense against a bear. Always remember to make sure of your target 100 percent and what is beyond it. Don't assume it's a bear you hear in the brush. You must confirm this! The noise could be a deer, moose, elk, or even another person. Safety must always be first in mind when hunting no matter what weapon you're using. Just a friendly reminder.

Know your target and what is beyond it. Ask yourself what is beyond your target. That arrow or bullet will likely keep going through the animal, so be prepared and know where it is headed. Think safety because you cannot call a bullet or arrow back.

If you can afford a good spotting scope, that will give you a slight edge over not having one. Now you can glass from a greater distance, across a valley or mountainside, and cover lots of ground you would otherwise have to see by hiking to it. Take your time glassing, and pick apart the landscape. Bears do not hide like a deer would, for example, but they still stay in brush a lot, and this will conceal the bear even if it's walking around. Focus your glassing efforts in the mornings, late afternoons, and early evenings. If you see a bear in the evening, you might not have time to chase after it that day, but you will likely have a decent idea of where it is hanging out on the next day. Provided there is food and it doesn't get blown out of the area by your scent or other factors, it might still be within your range. I have seen bears at different times of the day, but evenings have always been most productive. Another reason why I like to chase bears is that I can sleep in a little bit and head out for them in the afternoon with a generally good success rate. Target creek beds, berry patches, and other local food sources when you glass. Pay attention to your maps and GPS to find creeks or other bodies of water that might have brush close by.

My brother Jim and I hiked way up to a gorgeous mountainside bowl years ago with ten- to fifteen-foot nobles and Douglas firs scattered along the bottom, along with various brush such as devil's club and so on. The bowl was about a mile across. It was a hot mid-afternoon by the time we arrived. We were just enjoying the view as the evening progressed. As dusk approached, we were blessed with being able to watch several bears materialize in that bowl. (We didn't have a spotter scope—just some binoculars.) Some bears stood on their hind legs while watching another bear in the distance eating various berries. It was an amazing scene to watch a bowl come alive with five bears that we could see, let alone those we could not. Ah, the joys of hunting. Great memories with the family. It was a great example of how bears can remain hidden in cover easily. It was also a good reminder that if you have the patience to hold still and watch, you just might see something you would have otherwise missed. As with any hunting, you need patience.

When you purchase your spotter scope, do not forget to also get a good tripod. Many come with some sort of stand, so it should not be an issue; however, without a sturdy stand, long-range spotting is difficult, if not impossible. You can find adapters that connect to your vehicle's door if you choose. Take the time before the season to get to know your optics and gear. Teach yourself the ins and outs of the spotter, how to focus, how to scan broad areas from afar, and how to pinpoint something of interest quickly. When spotting bears, you might only see them briefly as they work their way through brush patches or tree lines. Be mindful of the weight of the item and tripod if you are going to be backpacking into a hunting area. Also, pay close attention to how you look through the optic before you buy it. Is it a straight shot to look through the scope or is the eyepiece angled? I have personally preferred spotting scope optics that have a straight body, not those with an angled eyepiece. That is just me—be sure to try it out thoroughly before purchasing such an item. You don't want to spend a bunch of money on a product like a spotter scope and then get buyer's remorse.

In this picture, you can see a lot of area, both close and far. This makes it an ideal spot to watch for bears and make a stalk.

If you shop around, you will find spotting scopes in different price ranges and magnifications. Depending on the terrain you hunt, they can be very handy. You will have to come up with your own excuse to tell your significant other why you spent so much on optics; I can't help you there. But what I can help you with is to urge you to decide what the best scope for you is and how to find it. First, you need to understand what the numbers on the spotter scope mean. It is quite simple really. A typical spotter scope number might read as follows: 20-60 × 65mm or 30-70 × 95mm. In these two examples, the 20-60 and 30-70 (the numbers to the left of the "×") equal the power, or magnification capabilities, of the scope. This simply means that whatever you are looking at through the scope will appear that many times closer than if you were to look at it with your naked eye. The numbers to the right of the "×" (65mm and 95mm in these examples) refer to the diameter of the objective lens in millimeters, which is the lens facing the target.

Spotting scopes are either fixed or variable in power. The fixed models are just that, fixed—they are set at a permanent magnification level and cannot be adjusted. Variable power means you can adjust the power of magnification between the specific numbers of that model. Spotting scope objective lenses vary in range size from about 50mm to 80mm. The bigger the number before the mm, the bigger your field of view with the scope will be—and likely the bigger the price tag.

Then you run into the different coatings that are available on spotter lenses. The different chemical coatings are used to help reduce glare and increase the amount of available light during low-light conditions. When only a single layer is applied to at least one lens surface, it is referred to as "coated" and this is like a base model. A "fully coated" scope refers to a single layer of coating applied to all air-to-glass surfaces, whereas a "multicoated" scope has multiple layers applied to at least one lens surface. Finally, a "fully multicoated" scope has multiple layers applied to all air-to-glass surfaces. This is a feature you would find on an upper-scale scope. Obviously, the more coatings you have on the scope, the more expensive the process to make the scope is, and therefore the cost of the scope is greater overall.

A few members of my family have spotter scopes that cost more than what I paid for my car. I am not sure if that says much about my car or too much about the scope! Everyone always says buy the best you can afford for optics, whether they are talking about rifle scopes, binoculars, or spotters. The more expensive, the better the view, the less eye fatigue, and so on.

Bears don't hold still much, so when using a spotter from a great distance, you might find it a bit hard to remain on target. Following a moving target with a spotter scope can be challenging. This is another reason why I like to use my binoculars; plus, where I hunt, it is typicallly a bit tough to see long distances, and so most of my spotting is a couple hundred yards at best. There are times when I will spot and stalk in the eastern part of the state, where the spaces are more open, hotter (or much colder depending on the time of year), and present their own challenges, all of which I welcome. When I am there, I am glassing across canyons into timbered bowls with creeks running on either side or down into brushy draws from the ridgetops with the right wind. The area is much more open, but the key to stalking is using what you have locally to block your movements.

I was able to hunt black bears in Alaska this past year for the first time, and I only had my binoculars with me. Though a spotting scope would have been useful to get a better idea of a few of the bears I was looking at, the binos I had worked well for the conditions and terrain. Additionally, I was limited to the weight I could carry due to the bush plane weight limits, so I brought along what I was used to and what I felt would be the most beneficial for the situation. Take your upcoming hunting situation into account when deciding if you are going to bring your spotter or another style of optic.

Sometimes spotter scopes must give way to the less powerful binoculars due to fog, limited sight distance, or general terrain.

But, for example, when hunting a more open area—it doesn't matter if it's a mountain meadow, open hillside, or a fresh clear-cut—you need to learn to use what you have available. If there are no trees to block your movements, use brush. If it is open grass that you have to traverse, are there any small draws or dips in the landscape you can use to your advantage? Are there any large rocks or other objects that will block your movements? The type of weapon you are using makes a big difference, too, since thirty yards is ideal for a bow, but depending on your skill with your rifle, you can be several hundred yards away from a potential ursine target. Timing is key.

Watch the bear's movements, and move when it eats with its head down or while it is tearing into a stump or otherwise distracted. If it's making a bunch of noise (and is therefore in a comfortable state) while moving about, time your noisy movements with this. Believe it or not, I have used jet noise to help cover my sound while trying to close the distance while elk hunting with my bow. The point here is learn to adapt to your situation and overcome the obstacles and challenges presented to you. Remember, patience is key. Luck doesn't hurt, either. Another trick I use is to make my noisy movements when the winds picks up; this helps blend the sound in and not make it so obvious.

There are lots of types of bear sign to pay attention to. Scat, tracks, torn-up stumps, dens, hair, game trails, bear brush tunnels—these are all clues to watch out for while searching for a good bear spot. Don't forget to keep an eye out for those stripped trees I wrote about in the preseason scouting chapter, as well.

Before you find an area you want to glass, make sure to take the wind into consideration. The wind will be blowing down a hill into a canyon in the early morning and then will switch to blowing uphill a bit due to the thermals brought on from the

Here are signs that bears frequent the area, but you have to judge how recent they are. Look for further sign, such as scat or prints in mud puddles.

change in temperature, generally speaking. This isn't always the case, but get to know the wind currents in your area and how they change throughout the day. Winds will be less predictable in some mountainous regions due to the terrain. If you spend enough time hunting in an area, you will likely get to know which way the prevailing winds blow. Slow down and take notice of the elements around you, as they can work for or against you. Slow down, be observant, take

it all in, and enjoy it. Really
getting into the zone of hunting takes a bit of time. Sometimes, it takes me a good hour
or more of walking before
I feel like I am really paying attention to everything
around me. Half the time, I
am so excited I am out hunting that I feel like I have to
rush to do whatever it is I am
trying to do. Take some time
to physically and mentally
slow down your movements.
You will be more successful
this way.

Let's say that you have
found a nice area and spotted a bear across a canyon
about equal to your current
mid-hill elevation with a
creek at the bottom. What to
do? Well, watch for a short
time and determine if it is
a bear you are willing to go
after. Are you looking for

Although it's hard to make out, this was a beehive that was in a burned-out tree's root system. The bear found the yellow jacket nest and proceeded to destroy it. By the time my boy and I found it, the bees were barely hanging on, but still a few remained. This was a great spot to set up for glassing for bear once we got out of the trees. Investigate hillsides or other spots you find dug up. You never know what the story will tell you.

a color-phase bear or just any legal bear? Does it have a big blocky head
or low-hanging belly? Does it walk around like it owns the place? Blocky
heads, a confident strut, small ears, and low hanging (fat gut) bellies are
often indicators of mature boars. Do the front legs look long and lanky or
are they shorter looking with a bulky chest? Is it in a spot that you can put
a stalk on? Are their cliffs and rocky areas that will block your stalk or allow
you to get above the bear for a shot? For this situation, we will say you want
to go for it.

Is the bear eating or resting in the sun? From my experience, the bear
is moving somewhere and rarely holding still except maybe for a nap or to
eat off a bush. Perhaps the bear is milling around out in the open and side-
hilling toward a brushy gulley that has some mature trees in it. Study the

area and try to pick an ambush spot. Where would you like to intercept the bear? Maybe there is a good ambush point on the other side of the draw.

Now, many people will attack this situation with different strategies than I might, but here is how I would do it (that is, if I weren't going to call it with a predator call, which would be my first choice). Before you leave your vantage point, find an easily identifiable landmark, such as a large rock, fallen tree, brightly colored bush that sticks out, a log landing—anything that will allow you to keep eyes on where the bear should be on your way down.

Provided the wind is in your face, head downhill (keeping tabs on the bear and your landmark) quickly but quietly depending on how far you have to go. Try to keep your movements hidden by using tree lines or lining up with objects to keep them between you and the bear so it is difficult for the bear to spot you. As you head down the hillside, try to position yourself ahead of where the bear will be. You don't want to come out right below the bear, as there is more of a chance to spook it; rather, try to come out just slightly ahead. Once you get to the bottom of the valley and have to cross the creek, it is very possible that the creek will cover some of your sound as you get past the brush that will likely line the creek. The wind may have changed now that you are at the bottom of the valley—perhaps a crosswind has kicked in or the wind may be going uphill toward the bear. Try to stay downwind of the bear as much as possible because if it smells you, it's more than likely long gone. Remember, you will not fool a bear's nose. If you have some wind-indicator powder, give a few puffs and see what it tells you, then adjust accordingly. You may want to keep this powder handy now that you are getting closer to the time to shoot.

Say you get across the creek and are slightly up the canyon from the bear. Keep working your way up the hill quickly but quietly. The closer you get to where you think the bear will be, the slower you should go. Remember, if you start to get close and it is difficult to remain quiet (due to dry conditions on the ground you are walking), try using a cow call or another local animal's call, such as a deer, to help cover your sound. Also be fully aware that the bear very well might come to that sound.

Now, let's say the bear headed into the brushy draw—now we have the problem of where the bear will go once you lose sight. The stalk can go any which way from this point. The bear could head down the draw to the creek (which is very possible on warm days), continue on the side of the hill, or decide it wants to head up the draw. Finally, it might just bed down. This is where you need a little luck.

Even I can blow a stalk now and again. This bear lived to see another day.

If the bear stays in the draw and you can hear him making noise feeding, you can either wait or give a few calls on your predator call if you have one. This will often break a bear loose of the brush and allow for a shot. Make sure you are not silhouetted but are hidden by some brush or a tree—something to break up your profile. It is likely the bear will be searching for that noise once you start. Of course, if the bear is already enjoying a food source, he may very well not care one bit . . . which I've experienced! If you don't want to try calling or you don't have a call, you can carefully work your way down into the draw to see if you can find the bear. Take your time with this—a few slow steps at a time listening carefully as you go. Work your way to the tree or brush line and remember to look low. Bears are not that tall when they are on all fours. You are likely to see parts of the bear rather than the whole bear when you first spot something. I don't know how many times I've been watching brush only to see a black paw pop out of the brush and grab a bundle of berries while never seeing the whole bear until later. Again, make sure of your target; don't see black and assume it is the bear. Be 100 percent sure of your target and know what's beyond it.

If the bear heads down-canyon, you can try to outmaneuver it, by heading to the bottom of the draw and keeping yourself hidden from view using the terrain to shield you as best you can. You might be able to

Note in this picture how you do not see the entire bear but only parts of the bear. This was taken when I could see the sow the best.

intercept the bear as it pops out of the brush, or you can get the bear while it heads to the creek to cool down. If you have a good view from where you are, you can watch to see where the bear goes into the creek bottom. Or try to position yourself so you are above the bear as it goes down into the creek bottom, and maybe there is a large rock along the draw you could set up on. Remember, you're not following a script, and bears will do what they want, which can be frustrating at times. But that's why we call it hunting, not shooting. The actions of bears, for the most part, seem fairly random with the exception of when they are looking for food or the opposite sex. Remember to use the animal's need for food as its Achilles' heel. It's a big weakness for them, and the later the season gets, the more intense the need for food becomes and the easier it is to exploit this trait. Winter is coming, and they know it. They have to try to pack on pounds as quickly as possible.

If the bear decides to continue moving along the side of the hill, hopefully you are close to the same elevation as the bear, and hopefully the wind is still in your favor. Try to position yourself within a comfortable shooting range, which depends on your weapon. If I am using a bow, I would try to tuck myself into a tree line or hide behind a bush to break up my movements. Hopefully, the bear will stroll along and present a good broadside shot. The bear might not, however, so you will want to be prepared to put on a different stalk, or you can make a lip squeak to get the bear's attention.

If the bear doesn't present itself for a good shot and it didn't seem to care about your lip squeaking, let it walk a little bit. Now you can try to go farther up the hill, just sixty yards or so, and try to move along the side of the hill with it to get ahead of it again—as long as the wind will let you. This way, you will be coming from above the bear and getting in a good ambush position. Hopefully, you can anticipate where the bear is heading, set up, and wait for it so you can drill it nice and clean. This could be a risky situation, though, so consider your options. I can write a million words on this, but the best way to learn this is to get out and try it.

Consider trying to stalk bears with your camera in the off season. If you can do it with your camera, you can do it with your bow or rifle, but bring some sort of protection with you, such as bear spray, a gun, etc. Bears are unpredictable, dangerous, very powerful, and curious animals, which are all reasons why I love them. These are also all good reasons to respect the animal and allow it space when the situation calls for it. If you are chasing them in the off season with a camera, just be sure to give them the space they deserve. There is no reason to create a dangerous situation for you and the bear for a picture. Far too often I see or hear of situations where people want to get a good picture of a bear, so they get too close and the bear charges or the bear gets crowded. These situations can be avoided completely.

Do not be discouraged if you mess up a stalk. Everyone does it from the world famous hunters to the beginner. Some just start to get better odds than others. I have had a rogue swirl of wind bust me I don't know how many times. That lone lead cow of an elk herd, oh man (my fellow elk hunters, you know what I am talking about), how I loathe that cow! I think I am close and then—"*BARK!*"—the cow, under some shaded tree on the outskirts of the herd that I didn't see, spotted my movement. All I can do is hold motionless and hope the elk go back to feeding and become relaxed. They usually do if they don't smell you—and of course it is about fifteen minutes later of holding absolutely still, usually in a position that is hard to hold, like one leg up and the bow in one hand slightly raised, my muscles screaming by the time I can readjust. The point is, smile and have fun with it regardless of your prey. Learn from your mistakes and, hey, now you have a story to tell, successful or not! You will get busted and you will fail, but with persistence, you will ultimately succeed.

There are certain tricks people can use to help get closer to bears or prey animals in general. Again, this depends on what type of weapon you are using and how far you are going to shoot. Even in wide-open areas, I rarely take shots of more than 100 yards with my rifle (most of my shots are fifty yards or less) not because I cannot make the shot (my rifle is sighted in at 200 yards), but I usually end up getting fairly close to the animal either by stalking or using a predator call. If you are using a bow, you need to be within a nice close bow range. Personally, I am looking for a thirty-yard or less shot with a bow. One trick I like to use is to wear a lighter boot or, once you get within stalking distance, to remove your boots and pack, which allows you to lighten your step and your socks can quiet your footfalls. Make sure you remember where you dropped your gear, though! Maybe take a second and mark on your GPS, if you have one available, where you placed your items. Personally, I am not one to take off my shoes too often, so there are alternatives to this, as well. They do make felt pads that attach to your boot to soften your sound as you walk along. For example, Wayne Carlton makes a product called Cat Paw, available at www.waynecarlton. com for around thirty bucks. This is an option for those of us who don't want to lose our boots miles back in the woods when putting on a stalk. Check your state regulations, though, to make sure these are legal where you hunt.

You will see some people crawl on the ground and peek over edges or ridgetops where they expect their quarry to be. This is not a bad idea at all and is one I have used. However, it is easy to silhouette yourself on a skyline and give away the position you worked so hard to gain when cresting a hilltop. The human form silhouetted is hard to mistake. As you crawl or sneak, don't just pay attention to your body as you go, pay special attention to your weapon so it doesn't fling a branch back and cause extra movement, get caught on a bush, or so forth. These tricks seem like common sense, but in the heat of the moment, when you are so focused on an animal and how to get to it, you might rush. Take a deep breath, relax, and focus on what you are doing, what the wind is doing, and what you must do to seal the deal.

Another trick I have used over the years when stalking prey is to walk like a deer—meaning to walk light, smooth, and slow through woods. Next time you get the chance, watch how a deer walks when it is browsing. It is slow, deliberate, and quiet for the most part. It is not one foot after another in a rhythm (unless it is headed out of the area), it is a step or two and then a pause. Try to imitate this as you go. Have your footfalls be as quiet as possible. Lay your foot down on its edges as you walk. Don't walk in a normal human pace or cadence, where a sound of footsteps would be "thump, thump, thump" as you plow down a road . . . an obvious human sound. Instead, as you travel, take a step and pause. Listen, take another step, and pause. These tactics will help you as a hunter get closer to your bear.

Remember, you might not have to go over the ridge and across the canyon to find a bear. If you have fresh sign nearby like bear scat, maybe you should take a good look around at your local surroundings first.

Watch where your foot will land and keep an eye out for sticks and leaves or other objects that will make noise. If you are going to land on a stick, try to keep your full weight off it, so as to not break it. Walk along the edges of roads or trails, not down the middle of them. It is harder to make out what you are if you are on an edge of a road or trail than if you are in the middle. Plus, there could be grass on the edges of the trail or road to help quiet your footsteps. Your silhouette can easily give you away. Walk on larger rocks to muffle your sound and use moist grass along roads to help keep you quiet. These are all basics of hunting, but they can really help you to close the distance on your bear. If you have stalked to an ambush position, are waiting for the bear, and have some time before it is going to show up, clear the ground around you a bit of twigs and leaves or anything that might give you away with sound as you position yourself for a shot. When I hunt elk in my normal ambush spot, I always clear a path so I can readjust my position with the least amount of noise possible.

In my younger years, I was deer hunting and came upon what we call in deer camp One Buck Hill. It is usually good for one buck a year, whether we get one in camp or someone outside of camp bags it. One buck per season— no more, no less. Tucked at the base of a canyon and a huge mountainous steep terrain packed with shale, it is a mule deer paradise. Not to mention the glorious white mountain goats that come down off the hillsides to drink out of the river that slowly cuts a sharp valley down the center of the timeless mountainside.

If you find a grove of trees that have been stripped like this or perhaps have been stripped the year before, you should try to get to a ridgeline and glass into any clearing around it or edge lines. Bears will work on younger trees in the spring, so you can use this behavior to your advantage. This tree was stripped one week before the picture was taken, and I was there when it happened.

As I rounded the corner of the trail one season to see the hill in question, sure enough, One Buck Hill remained true to its name. Standing tall was a gorgeous mule deer proudly looking down the hill at the ice-cold river that ran below. I had to close the distance to the majestic deer, as I thought it seemed a bit farther than I wanted to shoot. In my haste, I rounded the corner and was now blocked by trees and the noise of the river. I crossed the river using a log bridge and came up to the base of the hill by trudging through some chest-high brush. Buck fever had set in, and I was rushing the scene. The buck was nowhere to be found; probably it disappeared into the charcoaled tree line from a fire the area had sustained a few years back. I dejectedly went back to the corner vantage point where I first saw the deer, as I hoped to catch a glimpse of it. It was gone, of course, and after marking where the deer was standing with my range finder, I found it was only 220 yards, an easy shot with my rifle. But I blew the stalk . . . with my haste. I got excited, and I didn't think it through. Take your time. Still, I will never forget how pretty that scene was, of the buck standing on that hill looking over its territory, how the brush had turned to a red, yellow mesh, the river below was rushing, clouds were being torn by the mountain peaks above me, and the early morning air was fresh, cold, and clean. Totally worth it. In reality, I intend on having my ashes tossed into this valley when I die. I can think of no place better than this to be my final resting spot. The point of this is try to contain your excitement when you stalk if at all possible. Really just focus on the task at hand, be it making it to a tree for cover, closing the distance, or lining up an ambush. Don't get overwhelmed by the entirety of the situation; break it down to smaller goals to help complete the main goal of bagging a bruin!

Bear are a lot like deer and elk in the respect that I have found them to be most active during the early morning and evening hours, particularly during the heat of summer. This changes a bit as the seasons change, as the later in the year it gets the more the need to fatten up for winter becomes urgent. Use this to your advantage, but hunt when you can, as well. Don't think that since it is the middle of the day you should not go out hunting, especially if it is your only time to make it out. You likely will not find a bear by sitting in your living room—you have a much higher chance of getting one out in the woods.

Bears like to travel on the easy path. If there is a fallen log that offers safe and easy passage, bears will use it. The same can be said of old logging roads or hiking trails. If you can look down or glass over to these areas, you should.

Make sure that if you are staying out until dark, you keep a close watch on the end of shooting time. While bears do tend to come out right at evening, it might not always be legal to shoot. Pay attention to this detail and give yourself some wiggle room; maybe quit five minutes before the end of shooting time so you don't spot one and risk taking a shot that might get you a ticket or worse. I will usually do this when I hunt, as I feel it is not worth the risk.

Late August 2015, I was out bear hunting in a favorite spot. It had been a very dry year, so many of my normal hunting areas, which are private timberland, were closed due to fire danger. Don't ask me how I am going to start a fire by walking in, but regardless, they were closed. So, I headed to some Department of Natural Resource (DNR) land, which was open. I hiked into a spot I had called in a bear the previous year.

It was a leisurely hike that late afternoon, which I rather enjoyed while I munched on fresh sun-warmed blackberries, a favorite of mine when I hunt bears. I worked my way up the logging road, which had some thick replanted tree areas on either side, chock-full of berries, and settled on the same logjam I had been on before. The smoke from the multiple fires in eastern Washington had left a rich smell of burning wood hanging low in the air with a smoky haze on a day of otherwise clear-blue sky. A small chipmunk, which may have never seen a human, sat not five feet from me, grabbed a blackberry, and enjoyed an early evening snack while perched on a limb. I didn't call in anything that evening, but I still greatly enjoyed just sitting there sharing the moment with the little chipmunk.

Darkness was fast approaching, and the sun was sitting low past the tall Douglas fir skyline. The sky was an eerie orange and red with the light filtered from all the smoke. I decided to walk slowly on the way out, as I had another forty-five minutes at a brisk walk to get to the truck. While there was plenty of food, water, and cover, I hadn't noticed much in the way of bear sign, which was surprising—with the exception of some brush that had been beaten up by a bear, who obviously was enjoying the berries as much as I was. I walked slowly and took my time down the crunchy gravel road.

I soon came into a shaded dark stand of timber inhabited by my blood-sucking nemesis: a swarm of mosquitos. They harassed me as I slowly walked, but soon they forced a quickened pace, as I was none too keen to be eaten alive. This particular night, I was just wearing a T-shirt, so I was easy pickings. I paused for only a second when I noticed a culvert that still had some water coming though it and a small amount of mud around.

I looked down to see if I could find any tracks. As dry as the year had been, any water or moisture was definitely worth checking out.

No sooner had I looked up when a decent-sized black bear bounded across the gravel road in two leaps. He was fat for this time of year, which didn't leave much room between the ground and his belly. Now, the past year I called to a good-sized bear who left a clearing and hung up in the woods at about twenty yards; I wondered if this was the same bear. There was no way to tell for sure, but he was within a few hundred yards of where I had called the year before.

As the bear disappeared into the woods on the side of the road, I was not sure if it had heard me drudging down the road on the gravel or if it was just by chance that we literally crossed paths. I pulled out my predator call from RR calls and gave it a quick yet quiet blow, as I hoped to cause the bear to slow or perhaps pop back out. I worked my way to the spot where he crossed and decided to head into the brush after the bear, as it was kind of open in the trees—open enough for a thirty to forty yard shot, at least. I crashed through some brush, tried to get up the embankment, and huffed like a threatened bear. So far, I wasn't sure if the bear left or if it was very close. I huffed and popped my teeth trying to tree the bear or at least get a reaction.

Turns out, the bear was about forty yards in, if that, and busted up some brush as I got closer; I never did get another good second look. My point for all of this? Well, I thought it was a decent story, but more importantly I wanted to show that, as with any hunting, things can happen quickly, and just because you don't see a ton of sign around doesn't really confirm that there are no bears. I had seen bears in the area year after year, usually coupled with a lot of sign. I had a great suspicion that bears were still in the area despite the fact that there was not an overabundance of sign. The area had all bears needed—food, area to roam, cover, and, important that year, water. My theory was confirmed, and so was my Grandpa O's saying, "Let's take off while we still have a little light. You never know what you might see." I am all for staying until dark, but my usual way of doing things is to leave while I have a little light in which to see.

The trick I spoke of with huffing and popping my jaws was something I am trying to perfect from the legendary Jim Shockey, bear hunter *extraordinaire*. He has some great hunting videos, as well as TV shows, which are always a kick to watch. While he usually does wear his telltale black cowboy hat while bear hunting (something I do not recommend for safety reasons), he certainly knows bears and bear behavior and does a ton for hunters worldwide. I have watched him tree a few bears this way and am looking forward to when I get one treed using this trick! So, thanks for the tip, Jim Shockey.

If I were able to tree this bear, I could have judged him more closely and seen whether I wanted to shoot the bear or let it pass. Since I had already taken a spring bear that year from a special draw hunt in May, I was more selective about the second and final bear of the year. In late August, it is still very warm and the hides are not prime yet. That is what I am looking for—a larger bear with a prime coat. I would really like my stepson to be along with me when—or if—I take another bear this year, since he had put forth the effort with me earlier but wasn't with me when I shot the first bear. Naturally I want the meat, too, but hides are important to me.

One of my favorite finds out in the woods (other than any sheds I come across) was this sun-bleached bear print on a log I happened to be sitting on while deer (and bear) hunting. I didn't notice it until I got up to leave. The bear had stepped on it with wet paws, and it had basically baked into the log. Pretty incredible. Notice the claw marks that extend out from the paw pad imprint. These were scratches in the log, and there was no dirt on the log from the print at all.

When you are spotting and stalking bears, take the time to ensure it is a bear that you want—unless you are just trying to get the first bear you have ever hunted. Any bear, or animal for that matter, to me is a trophy. I am not a trophy hunter; I do not need the biggest bruin or buck. I enjoy all my hunts. I am proud of some does and cow elk I have shot, and they were extremely good eating! But if hide is important to you and you are trying to make a record book, take your time and get a good look at the animal. You don't want to tag out on a bear and be disappointed with ground shrinkage, which bears are famous for. If you have never shot a bear, you might not be familiar with that term "ground shrinkage." It refers to seeing a bear live on foot and thinking it is huge. Then you shoot the bear and walk up on it only to realize that you are dealing with a smaller bear. Bears are famous for being hard to judge in size and sex.

When you are sizing up a bear, pay special attention to the bear's ears. If they are small and off to the side of the head, the bear is likely a good size. If the ears are really tall and obvious near the top of the head, it is likely a smaller bear. Another important judgment to keep in mind is to make sure you know the difference between a grizzly bear and a black bear. Both can come in similar colors, and not all black bears are black. Pay attention to their faces. Grizzlies will have a flat, dish plate face, while black bears have a more pointed facial profile. The telltale hump on a grizzly's back is also a good clue to look for. Take the time to check out some videos online that show the differences between the two. It could save you from a fine or jail time. Take a look at the pictures provided here and compare the difference between the two animals even though they may be similar in color.

Photo by Justin Haug.

This is a grizzly bear. Notice the dish plate face and the hump on its back.

Photo by Justin Haug.

Notice the long muzzle on the black bear. Also notice how the bear is not black but is similar in color to the grizzly. Not all black bears are black! This bear also lacks the grizzly hump on its back. Do you see the difference in the ears, too? Know the difference between black bears and brown or grizzly bears.

Photo by Justin Haug.

Notice in this picture, again, the pronounced hump on the grizzly's shoulders. If you see a grizzly in the wild, it is best to keep your distance and make noise or allow the bear to smell you from afar so you don't startle it. Give yourself and the bear plenty of room.

Photo by Justin Haug.

The top of the food chain in North America is the absolutely wonderful and horrible grizzly bear. Make sure if you are in grizzly country that you are prepared not only to fend them off but also to be able to tell the difference between a black bear and a griz or brown bear. Black bears are not the only bears that enjoy green grass.

I remember as a kid going out hunting. I might bring a water bottle, maybe a snack or two in a pocket. Now that I am older and a bit wiser, I know the importance of hydrating and keeping fueled up. I know that since I have made the conscious decision to drink water frequently, I certainly feel better and hunt more efficiently. I remind you to do the same. Drinking water and other fluids that replenish the body as you spot and stalk are essential. CamelBaks are efficient ways to keep water readily available. Be aware of the weather and what the weather might do while on your stalk. Just a bit of advice.

Now, back to another scenario. Say there is an area where you have seen bears on your trail camera, but it is thick with brush. You know bears are in the area, but you are not sure how to get to them. The first thing you should ask yourself is why are the bears there (food most likely), and where are they going? There is a food source in the area they are likely hitting. If you are getting pictures in the early spring and the bears disappear, then the food source likely did, too. If you are getting pictures in the summer and they seem to hang around until the fall, then you have yourself a decent area.

Find a trail that bears are using frequently. This may be a bear brush tunnel, as well, depending on how thick it is. If you are able, follow the trail for a bit and get to know it, where it leads, discover if there are bigger openings where you can sit and wait for an ambush, or if there is a water hole nearby. One option might be that the bears are entering the brushy area for food but come from a timbered area close by or work the edges of a clearing on their way to the area. Hang back and watch for travel routes to and from the area. If you watch these routes and nothing shows up, change strategies. If you do catch some bears going to and from these routes, then you know what to do. Get yourself in position to make a stalk on the bear in a less thick area if at all possible.

Another option that can work for this scenario is to clear brush with some clippers to try and capitalize on the area the next season or perhaps in the current season if you are lucky. By making a clearing or paths that you know of, you might just have that area to yourself as far as hunters go. Bust into the brush a good fifty or eighty yards, so it is difficult to see the clearing or path you are making. Then, decide where you want to place the paths or clearing. Since, from your entrance point, you cannot really see the clearing area, other hunters will likely just walk on by thinking it is too thick. All the while you are buried in bear-hunting paradise. Also, if the situation calls for it, use a tree stand or blind to try to change your luck in thick areas. I know this section is about spotting and stalking, but you must be able to adapt to your hunting areas and use what works best.

How about hunting with a partner? Now you can use the bear's nose to your advantage. A bear is down a hill that you are glassing with your hunting buddy. Let's say it's grazing on some springtime grass in an opening that is lined by ravines on either side of the bear. The wind is blowing across and down from your position to the bear, who is about 400 yards off. So you are above the bear, and the bear will likely smell you soon unless you act. One of the hunting party needs to try to get upwind of the bear slightly so the bear will be less likely to catch human scent. The other hunter should try to work around to underneath the bear (unless an overhead ambush position presents itself) or near-likely cover the bear will head to once spooked.

The idea in this situation is for one hunter to stay above the bear while the other works to an ambush position below. Once the hunter who stays above the bear can see the other hunter in position (or after a set amount of time), he or she can use the wind to cause the bear to smell them, and the bear will likely head for cover; it could move fast or just wander off. This is risky, and a side or overhead ambush would likely be better, but having options never hurts. Allowing a bear to smell you with another hunter in position is similar to that of a deer drive and might work great in some situations.

Remember to play the wind to your advantage as much as possible with bears, as their nose is a major defensive protection they possess.

In this picture, notice the claw marks and how they are close to the track. This indicates a black bear track and not a grizzly. Always be on the lookout for various types of bear sign when you are hunting. It can give you an idea of where bears are and where they are headed. With grizzly tracks, the claws will extend much farther away from the body of the toes on the track than those of a black bear. Check to see how fresh the track is by how well defined it is. The more defined and sharp the track, the fresher it is.

So this will completely depend on what you are looking for. But I wanted to give an example of a bear that has been "rubbed." A bear will come out of its winter den with a full coat for the most part. It might have a rub mark on its side or butt from being in the den, but generally, springtime is one of the best times to get a prime hide. When they come out and start looking for food and the weather gets warmer, they start to scratch and rub as a way to cool down. When you are spotting bears for a stalk, you might want to pay special attention to this when you are sizing up your bear if the hide is important to you. As for me, I have kept all of my bear hides; I love them, and I think they are a great addition to my man cave. Just be aware that you might want to wait until you get a good 360-degree view of the bear before you decide to commit to putting on a full-on stalk.

There are some essentials you should have with you when you go out for a spot-and-stalk hunt. I am going to give you a list of what I basically carry for a day's hunt. This is not an all-out perfect list, but this is a list that works for me.

Photo courtesy of Justin Haug.

This is probably one of the ugliest bears I have ever seen. Not only is the poor fellow covered in what we call "goat heads," a sticky seed, but the hide is rubbed all over the buttock area and its right shoulder. This is a bear you would definitely pass on if you were looking for a quality hide.

GEAR LIST

1. Tag, licenses, and weapon with clip and ammo
2. Bow, release, and arrows if you are hunting that way; I usually don't carry a bow repair kit—I just wax down my string before I go out—but they do make some nice compact repair kits
3. Backpack with full waterbottle
4. Knife set (I have switched to the Havalon Hydra), bone saw, and three breathable meat bags
5. First-aid kit with ibuprofen, quick clot, different gauze, tape, and a SPOT emergency transmitter
6. Parachute chord, which always comes in handy; I usually have fifty feet or so
7. Water purifier (I use a Steripen)
8. Snacks and a package of freeze dried food, plastic fork
9. Jet boiler with cup and fuel
10. Waterproof matches, lighter, flint, fire starter (i.e. dryer lint, cotton balls smothered in Vaseline; it is important to carry more than one way to start a fire in case something gets wet)
11. Compass, small reflective mirror for signaling during an emergency

12. Garmin GPS (don't forget to mark where you parked right before you leave so you will have a way point to where your vehicle is in case you get turned around; do not rely 100 percent on your Garmin, be aware of your surroundings, how you came in, and so on because Garmins are electronic and can fail on you; be prepared to use a compass if you need to)

13. Emergency thermal blanket (looks like a big sheet of tinfoil but works wonders when needed); don't skimp on this, buy a decent brand that is a little tougher than your average cheapo—you won't be disappointed if you need it

14. Toilet paper and a small baggy of baby wipes to avoid the dreaded monkey butt

15. Individual coffee bags, hot cocoa, and some flavored water powder packets

16. Extra gloves and hat

17. Extra batteries for the GPS

18. Hand predator call (of course!) usually around my neck, binoculars or spotting scope

That should about cover it for a day-hike pack. If I am backpacking into an area for a few days, this obviously changes, and I add extra socks, sleeping bag, and tent. One thing you always want to make sure you are doing is letting someone know where you are going and when to expect you back. I will often tell my wife if she doesn't hear from me by a certain time (usually the next morning), something is wrong. I try to always pack as if I am going to stay the night outside because one of these times, I might bust an ankle or who knows what and have to stay the night. Even if it is just a day hike, be prepared to stay out in nasty weather. Hypothermia is common, even in the summer, as people do not dress for changing conditions. If you get wet at night and you are up in the mountains, it cools down to the low sixties or fifties, and you cannot dry off or get warm by a fire, you could find yourself in trouble. As I write this, Washington hunters just lost one of their own—a guy who went out on a day hunt for late-season bow hunting. He was a former Marine and about fifty-five years of age, an avid hunter, but died due to a fall off an embankment (or so preliminary results suggest). My point is, accidents are just that, and you usually don't see them coming, so be prepared. By the way, rest in peace to the hunter who passed.

Day packs differ greatly from an extended stay-over hunt. Be sure to make a list, prepare, and double check your gear. Here is my bear camp in Alaska. Always be familiar with all of your gear before you go out for a long stalk camping trip. I usually completely set up my tent in the living room before packing it up for the trip to make sure it still works as intended.

If you are an experienced hunter, I am sure you have your own list. If you are new, this isn't a bad list to start with. You might want to add a few things or take out a few things, but it's a good start. There are Internet hunting-forum threads that are devoted to the topic of what to bring along on a day or overnight hunt.

Remember, when it comes to spotting and stalking black bears, the best strategy is to try to pick areas in which to spot and from which you can put on a stalk. You want to try to find slightly more open areas but areas that contain food sources. High-altitude mountain blueberry fields are great. Avalanche chutes, shale slides with pika in them, fresh green meadows in the springtime—all are good places to start to look for bears. If you deer or elk hunt, keep a mental or actual physical note of bear sign, good bear habitat areas, and so on. Keep your ears open for talk with other hunters about where bears have been taken, or maybe someone in deer camp has seen one—anything to give you that tip on where to start your spot-and-stalk adventure.

If you choose areas that are "stalkable," then you are likely to have a greater success rate. In all honesty, where I hunt usually is very thick with brush, but bears love it. If I think it is too thick to spot and stalk, I usually

Here's a small, but evidently satisfying, snack for a black bear. I was privileged enough to watch a bear gorge itself on several of these hapless victims once.

call into it. I change how I approach certain hunting areas due to what the terrain holds. Stick with environments that allow for plausible stalking situations. Take into account what you are hunting with, as well. If you want to try to spot and stalk thick areas with lots of brush, you might want to consider hunting with a shotgun instead of a bow. Really consider your gear and terrain carefully. Tailor your needs with what is being offered in the hunting area.

Take into consideration, as well, that your spotting scope can see in some cases a mile or more away, and that's the way the crow flies. It could be farther than that traveling by land. You might be looking across a deep canyon or several mountainsides at a bear on a sidehill and think you want to go for it. What time of day is it? Is there enough time to make it to the bear? Are there other objects in your way that you must traverse, such as a deep river, nasty crevasse, swamps, cliffs, glaciers, ice fields, and so on? Are you physically able to take such a hike with enough time to actually put a stalk on the bear? Will the bear even still be there by the time you get there, or is it moving along at a good pace? Will you be able to physically get the bear out of that location? Is it very hot outside or extremely cold? Is there a storm front coming in? All these are things to consider before even stepping foot on your journey to stalk the bear.

Not all sightings are miles away. Some are just down a ravine. I spotted a black bear while elk hunting in 2013 but decided to pass on even putting a stalk on it. While it was only 400 yards down a canyon, I would guess it was surrounded by elk and a few deer. The bear walked down a shale face and then started back up the canyon to an adjacent canyon while walking away from me. I was bow hunting, it was getting near dusk, and there were blowdowns and brush all over between it and me. I didn't have the time to mount a good stalk due to the brush, weapon, and time of day, not to mention the forty-some eyes and noses that were all over the hill. So, I watched the bear and let it go with the hope I could return in the next few days and try to get it. That was the last I saw of the bear that season, which was fine. It was still a blessing to see it.

Sometimes, bears just decide that you don't have to travel too far for a spot and stalk. This bear was waiting for me when I returned from a short hike. I waited about ten minutes or so before the bear decided to move on.

Bears are different from mule deer, elk, and so on. You cannot rely on them to bed down and hold still during midday. They just have a different pattern than ungulates, and they don't need to chew their cud. This is why it can be such a challenge to really be able to pinpoint bear behavior. The buggers just do what they want. Setting up for ambush points on moving bears, staking out their food and water sources, and glassing for bears are all strategies you will need to utilize if you are to be a successful spot-and-stalk bear hunter. If you have never tried to spot and stalk bear, I would really encourage you to give it a try—you will not regret it!

Chapter Five

Calling Bears

Well, this is a favorite topic of mine. Your wife will call you crazy, your friends will wonder if you have a death wish, and others will ask what the hell are you thinking, but you can laugh at all of them and get back to calling bears, a true sickness that takes over your hunting thoughts! Let me start off by saying that predator calling for any animal can be dangerous. You might call in a cougar, grizzly (depending on where you live), wolves, coyotes, bobcats, black bears, get dive bombed by hawks or eagles, or have any other hungry predator come to see what is for dinner. Elk will come charging in to see what the noise is (so it's not a bad way to call elk, by the way), and female deer will bound in huffing and stomping—they really like to make a scene. Be especially careful during the rutting season of animals. They are already not thinking clearly and are aggressive. Be warned, you can get hurt doing this. Of course, you can get hurt snowboarding, riding a roller coaster, or swimming. So, that being said, I say let's dive in! You have been fairly warned.

Predator calling, especially for black bears, is one of my favorite hunting pastimes. It is absolutely heart pumping to see a black bear, drooling and pissed off, come plowing through the brush ready to kill and eat whatever is making all that noise. Ever seen that in real life? It's better than a double shot of espresso with a red-bull topper. Since I am the one making the noise with a predator call, you can see why I would be excited. I am the one making all the noise and saying in animal terms, "I am dying, oh the agony, come and eat me!" Of course there is also the sneaky bear who wants to see what is making all that noise before pouncing on it. Turing your head and seeing a bear a few feet from you when you had no clue there was one there is also a heart stopper. I love it! It's crazy, it's dangerous, and most people in their right minds wouldn't do it. But I have never been accused of being in my right mind. To me, the ones you see coming are not the truly scary ones. No, the scary ones are the ones you don't see at all. I have had a few bears come in to check me out, a few as close as fifteen yards, and I never realized they were there until my hunting partner pointed it out after the fact. Tracks in the snow don't lie.

The very first time I ever predator called, I went to Sportsman's Warehouse and bought an AP6 Sceery brand closed-reed predator call. I drove up to a logged-off area I know of, drove up the mountain, parked down the road a bit, and hiked up to a logjam. I tucked myself into the logjam to blend in with it. I called in a coyote and bobcat and was instantly hooked. I didn't shoot either animal, as I was bear hunting, and the bob was out of season, anyway. But to sit and watch those animals sniff and look around for me was, frankly, incredible. I had never seen a bobcat in the wild before then, and I thought what a marvelous new hobby this is going to be. Years of hunting and never seeing a bobcat, and now thirty minutes of predator calling and I see one! Incredible. It was not just the fact that I was able to see the bob and song dog, it was the fact I had them *come* to me.

Photo courtesy of Justin Haug.

I called in this coyote in Alaska on a set under five minutes. The joys of calling—you just never really know what will come in and check you out.

Calling for bears is a perfect strategy if you are looking at an area and think there could be a bear around, but perhaps it is too thick to put a stalk on or it is a vast valley that presents a lot of ground to cover. Sound can cover it for you and save your legs. Let your lungs do the work, and have the animals come to you. I call in superthick areas all the time, as long as I can get high up so I can see what is coming in (well, even if I can't) and for safety reasons. But be prepared once you start calling, as animals can show up very quickly. I have had bears and coyotes show up in five minutes or less. This is all due to predator calling. I can promise most of you that once you get an animal coming into a call, regardless if it's a bear, coyote, cow elk all pissed off, doe stomping and huffing, or birds of prey, you will get hooked. Things happen quickly when calling. Be set up, and be ready with weapon in hand!

For those of you who live in states with thick brush or dense tree stands and are used to baiting or running with dogs, if you want to try something new or perhaps baiting has been outlawed, you should really give predator calling a try. Give it a good ten to fifteen stands. If you don't love it by then, try another set! Even if your hunting area is beset with lakes, ponds, rivers, thick trees, and other obstacles, calling is a great way to get the predator to come to you. I cannot overstate this. Like me, you might find yourself with a slight addiction to collecting different calls in a similar fashion to a fisher who collects lures. This one looks different, sounds slightly different, is a custom work of art made of elk antler—another unique call you just have to have. I am not endorsed by them, but I can attest to RRCalls.com for custom-made predator calls. I have bought several and called in several animals with all the calls I have purchased from them. In fact, my older brother David called in a wolf last winter with a call I gave to him as a gift. So, if you are looking for some unique types of calls, check out RRCalls. com; they will treat you right.

Swamps are a great place to call for bears. They usually offer cover, water, and an edge line where you can spot the bear coming in. Usually there is some sort of opening where you would be able to get a shot off. This photo was taken in the springtime; notice all the fresh green grass shoots coming up.

When I started to write this book, I was considering who I would want to comment on bear calling, and Wayne Carlton came to mind almost instantly. Wayne Carlton (www.waynecarlton.com) is a bear-calling personality who fascinated me when I first watched his DVD titled *Call'N Bears: They Come to Eat.* If you want an action-packed, informative DVD on what to expect when calling, this is it bar none. I highly recommend anyone interested in calling bears to check it out. Out of the blue, I emailed Wayne, explained my book, and asked if he would consider writing a little something about calling. Keep in mind, I am nobody famous—just a guy writing a comprehensive bear book to the best of my ability. To my very pleasant surprise, I got a response right away. Wayne was also generous enough to take his time and effort to share some of his bear-calling experience in this book. I was blown away by this. The knowledge he is willing to pass along is truly valuable—I personally know it—and I am very happy to bring this to you. I really hope you enjoy his brief writing. Trust me, this is bear-calling gold. The following is Wayne's input:

On this particular hunt we were actually spring turkey hunting upon the 'notellum' plateau, which is known for heavy populations of bears. The young fella that I had with me thought at the time that he had seen someone's horse, which would be unusual because the horses had not made their way up this high because of all the snow. I looked around the corner and could see the back of what I thought was a pretty good-size bear. I told the young man that it was not a horse but a bear, him being from South Carolina and having never seen a bear being called before, his adrenaline flow was ready to take off. We got within 100 yards of the bear as it was feeding off the grass like a cow would be feeding, with its back toward us.

Right here is where the tip comes in—I started calling with a triple-reed diaphragm call design for calling turkeys. It produces a rather raspy sound but I thought I would give it a try. I called several minutes and the bear would occasionally look up but he would not come in to the call in any manner.

Next, I tried a double-reed diaphragm that I normally use for calling out elk. This is a very high-pitched call and it creates some very high-pitched screams and squalls. After calling fairly hard for a minute or two, the bear finally picked his head up, looked in our direction, and started walking parallel left to right in front of us, but still did not show signs that he was going to come in our direction. At which time, I started squalling extremely loud, ear piercing like somebody was pulling my arm off and was going to beat me with it. Guess what the bear did? He forgot everything he was thinking about and he came running in, jumped up on top of a fallen aspen. He looked in our direction and as he did that I started calling as if I was on steroids.

The bear started running to us, which was absolutely beautiful since there was two inches of water that he was running through. As the bear got close I started toning it down and he slowed down. He got within twenty yards, at which time I quit calling the bear. He stopped coming in our direction and he started looking around to see where everyone had gone. I told him that I was a human and the guy with me had a gun and that we should probably quit, and that is what he did. So the tip here would be if you try one call that is not working switch to another call, I have found a higher pitch and more desperate sound, the more exasperated the sound, the better the success. When you're calling bears plan on having some patience. Occasionally, they will pick up and just run at you; other times they come very methodically.

If you would like to learn more about Wayne Carlton, check out his website at www.waynecarlton.com.

What did we learn from this story by Wayne? Let's dissect it and find out. Number one, the person who spotted the bear wasn't even sure it was a bear at all; he thought it was a horse (which was no fault of his own, he wasn't used to seeing bears). So, our first lesson is be sure of your target, and remember, you might only see part of a bear, such as a splash of black in the brush, a paw rising out to grab some blackberries, and so on. Regardless of this, be 100 percent sure what it is you are looking at. I cannot overstate this.

Number two, Wayne starts calling with a call that is designed for another style of hunting—it is not even a predator call. It is a turkey call. This can be a very good thing and is an excellent example of unconventional calling. The call is generally not used for bear hunting. Therefore, this might not be a sound the bear is used to hearing, so it might pique his interest. Or, if the bear has been called to before, it is likely it has not been educated to that sound, so it might come in not realizing it is a hunter calling rather than some wounded animal. In this case, the first call did not work that well for Wayne. The bear raised its head a bit but was more concerned about eating grass. So, what did Wayne do? He switched it up with another style of raspy call, again, something not used in traditional predator calling, an elk call. This is a very important point not to be missed. Unconventional calling works and works well when used properly. That's a bear-calling gold nugget right there.

Number three, the sounds he made were very high-pitched, frantic, and raspy squalls. They were not subtle and soft. Rather, they were loud, obnoxious, and attention-getting, and it apparently worked. Now, in this instance, I cannot always say that switching prey animal calls will work like this, but in this case, it was enough to pique the bear's interest and caused it to run into the call. The bear would have been a goner had it been in season or a target animal. His calling worked likely because it was not your typical sound that the bear may have heard before. I am sure the wind had to be right, too, but that is beside the point.

My final point I want to discuss is very important but often overlooked. Can you spot it before I talk about it? Go ahead and look, reread the story, I will wait. . . .

The final point is this: as Wayne called and called frantically, the bear came running in. As the bear got closer, Wayne started to tone down his calling, and the bear's pace matched it by slowing down. Finally, the bear got to be within twenty yards, at which time Wayne quit calling the bear. What did the bear do? It stopped. Do you see the correlation? The tempo of the calling can often dictate the speed of the response. If you call and call often and frantically, the bear will likely match that speed. If you stop calling, the bear will stop. Not 100 percent all the time, but I have observed this enough through personal experience and read enough stories on bears to know this to be true. Do not forget to listen to his last sentence, as well. Bears can come running at you or be methodical and slow. You must be cautious, aware, and ready. Calling is often unpredictable, which is what makes it so fun.

TYPES OF PREDATOR CALLS

There are three different ways to call something in: with a hand call, which is a call that you put up to your lips and blow; a diaphragm call, which goes into your mouth; or an electronic caller, which usually uses a remote and digitally sends out sounds of various calls of your choosing. For hand calls, there are two styles, closed reed and open reed. Closed-reed calls are great for beginners (and are still my favorite calls for bears), as all the user has to do is blow into the call using various different breath strengths for louder or quieter sounds. Biting the mouthpiece on these calls will also increase the pitch of the sounds, while just flat out blowing into a closed-reed call has it sounding raspier and more guttural. There is a disadvantage to those who use hand calls, however, and that is movement. You will often cup the opening of the call in your hand to simulate mouth movements by opening and closing your hand. Little things like this can blow a set (no pun intended), especially for cats, which really watch for movement when coming in. That is when FOXPRO comes in handy.

Those of you who hunt elk are probably used to diaphragm calls, small semicircle latex calls that you place on your tongue for hands-free operation. I am not a fan of these calls, as they seem to trigger my gag reflex. My brothers use them for elk, but they just are not for me. There are numerous brands of diaphragm calls to consider, but they do take a bit of practice to get used to. You might find yourself getting yelled at by your better half as you wander about the house blowing various calls. Of course, my wife would never do this to me . . . *cough* . . . nor would I ever tell my boy to quiet down after he finds some of my calls. . . . On second thought, you might want to hide your calls for your own sanity.

Open-reed calls are often found as coyote howlers with a flat reed exposed on the mouthpiece of the call. In this case, the user must wet the reed and then place it in their mouth. They use their upper teeth either closer to the tip of the reed to make a higher-pitched sound or further back on the reed (closer to the other end of the call) to make a deeper sound. Open reeds take a bit of practice, but they have their uses, for sure. I have called in bears using open-reed calls before as a pup-distress call. But again, for a beginner, I would suggest a closed reed. By all means, if you see a howler or open reed you like, pick it up and bring it along. An added call in the pack can help out or might produce the sound that breaks that bear loose of the brush. I usually stash a call in my vehicle's glove box, as well. You never know when you might need one!

Electronic calls or e-callers, as they are referred to, come in all shapes and sizes. They range anywhere from fifty dollars up to seven hundred or so. When I think of e-callers, the first name that comes to mind is FOXPRO. FOXPRO makes all sorts of e-callers for every budget. I started out with a Spitfire e-caller, an entry-level caller that is great for a beginner. I then came into the possession of the Inferno caller by FOXPRO. It comes with seventy-five preloaded sounds and the ability to have two hundred uploaded to it. The remote has an improved range over the Spitfire model, an easier and bigger screen display to read, and the sounds listed in categories. Finally, it has a feature called Fox Bang, which automatically switches calls at the sound of a gunshot, which could come in handy if you miss. Switching a screaming rabbit to that of a coyote bark or howl might just be what you need to help stop that bear from barreling out of town if you miss. This call is made in the USA, which nowadays is hard to find. I can honestly say, as far as e-callers go, FOXPRO has my business for life.

Along with the different e-callers from FOXPRO, you can get movement decoys that directly attach to the caller, such as the Fox Jack 2. It replaces the battery cover on your caller and provides crucial movement needed to really fool the predator (in this case, a bear) coming into the call. Adding movement is deadly for cats. It even has an LED for nighttime use, however, for bears we will not be using this feature, as it is illegal to hunt bears at night— at least where I hunt. The light feature is mainly aimed at bobcats and coyotes, predators you can hunt at night most of the time. My experience with FOXPRO has been second to none in both customer service and overall friendliness. I highly recommend them.

In this picture you can see all the different styles of calls from electric callers, like the glorious FOXPRO Inferno/Fox Jack 2 combo, to the closed-reed styles, open-reed howlers, and open-reed distress calls. You will soon find yourself with a large collection of predator calls, much like a fisher with lures.

Let's talk about your setup for calling. If you have watched any of Randy Anderson's, "Calling All Coyotes" by Primos videos, you know most predators come to a caller from downwind (another *must-have* video for any predator caller, by the way). They like to smell what they are coming to, naturally, for safety's sake. Smaller bears don't want to stumble on a bigger bear tearing into some hapless victim, for example. They could easily become the victim. Bobcats and cougars are the exception here. They are sight driven, not driven by smell, so if your goal is for cats, you have to remain as absolutely still as possible. They will focus on the movement of the decoy like a laser beam. It is really something else to see a cat come into a call that is moving. It's kind of scary, really.

Holding still for bears is important but not as important as it is for cats. Cats are very cautious and, worse yet, patient. We could only be blessed to be able to hunt like a cat. They will sit tucked in brush or a tree line and watch where they think the call is coming from for as long as it takes, and if they spot something they don't like, *poof* . . . bye-bye, kitty. They can also hide like no other animal. I had a cougar at thirteen steps behind me stalking me at night, and it was pressed flat against the ground just behind a fallen tree that was no more than a foot tall. I also never noticed how white a cougar's chin is until I saw its whole face in my scope as it laid

down, digging its rear legs in the dirt and getting ready to pounce. I was a little scared of the dark that night, let me tell you. In fact, my little brother, who was with me and who never swears, let out a few cusses when he spotted that cat right on us. Good times, and I really couldn't blame him! I let out a few myself.

So, let's say you have your best shooting lane downwind, meaning you have the wind at your back or blowing crosswind. Safety should be the first consideration. Have your back against a tree, stump, or rock—something solid. If you cannot rest against something, try to at least get higher up. Maybe on a tree stand, logjam, or even a rock outcropping that overlooks a valley or ravine. The idea is that an animal will not be able to hop on

It is important to pick your calling area carefully not only for safety but for success. Here I am searching the area before setting up for a calling session. Not only is down below me nice and wide open, but there is a ton of brush lining the valley floor providing plenty of spots for bears to hide out.

your back and snap your neck like a chicken. If at all possible, have a second hunter with you. Not only will this increase your safety, but you will have another set of eyes. Of course, this does increase your scent contamination in the woods, but you have to give a little to get a little. A second person is not necessary but can be helpful. I call alone plenty of times.

If you are calling with a hand call, have the second person slightly downwind of you or equal to you, far off to either side, or have them looking the opposite direction as you are fifty or seventy yards behind you. Keep each other in sight for safety reasons (so you do not aim toward one another). The idea is that the second hunter will catch something trying to sneak in from behind. If you are using an electronic caller, place it out fifty yards or more in front of you, preferably up high, such as on a hay bale, stump, or even a tripod. This will help get the sound out farther. As for any calling, remain as still as possible. Be sure not to silhouette yourself on a hill. It is best to try to tuck into the hillside to break up your outline.

This distance that you place the e-call at depends on the range of the remote for the call. Some are greater than others. If you are going with an electronic caller, do your research and find one that both fits your budget and your needs. There are plenty out there. Try to listen to them at the store if at all possible. On some cheap models, the sounds come out tinny sounding. You want loud, clear, crisp sounds.

Earlier I said how I prefer hand calls, and let me tell you why. (Except for cats—I'm for electronic calls for cats 100 percent, so I can hold still.) It is easier to come up with new sounds and new sound scenarios (for example, have a calf distress and then send out a coyote howl to create a situation that could actually happen) using a hand call or calls than it would be with an electronic call. Also, not all of them, but several calls you can get digitally have probably already been played by other hunters who have an electronic caller. Predators may have been educated already because of this. But if you have a few hand calls with you that sound different and make sounds that the predator has not heard before, it could be enough to spark the bear's interest. Also, don't hesitate to use both an electronic caller and hand caller. When used together, this combo could be deadly. Keep in mind you are trying to entice a bear to come and see what all the fuss is about. Often times, a new sound the bear has not heard before could be just the thing it responds to. The great thing about the FOXPRO Inferno is that you are able to record your own calling sessions on a computer and download them onto the caller.

So, you can have a bunch of sounds that you have made available on the electronic caller, which makes it a must-have for any predator caller.

I like to relate predator calling to fishing when I first introduce it to someone. Pretend you are in a boat and you see a sunken log a few feet below the water's surface on a nice, sunny summer morning. You would expect to find a bass or maybe some bluegills down there. Without a fish finder, what is the only way to find out? Cast a line down there and wait for the tug, which we all

A mountain valley is likely to contain bears, cougars, and all sorts of other critters. There is one way to find out what is hanging around down in there—cast a line out by calling, and see if you get any bites!

love! Predator calling is no different. If you are hunting and you see a nice brushy creek bed, you might think that a bear would be hanging around. And since they do not currently make bear finders like they do for fish, you have to cast out a line—or call down into that snarled mess and see what pops out. Just like with fishing, the more you cast or the more time you spend fishing, the greater the chance you will catch something. Calling bears is no different.

Now, it doesn't have to be a creek bottom, it could be a wide valley, a farmer's field with mature trees lining it, your favorite deer spot with the last bits of fruit rotting on the ground, or an area where you have seen bear sign before. Maybe you know of a spot where a buddy has seen bears or has been successful hunting bears; be open-minded on where to call, and try to think like a bear. The point I am trying to make here is you will never know what is out there until you call into it. Calling is a great way to cover lots of ground and get to know what is in the area. It is hard for me *not* to call into an area. Usually what stops me is I cannot set up with a shooting lane I like, or it is just too thick with brush and there is no way to get up high. Even still, I look for openings where I can use a shotgun and call.

A major consideration in addition to finding good bear habitats, safety of the caller, and a high probability of a bear being in the area is making it easy for a bear to come to you. Bears are a bit lazy, and it is best to make it

This is a perfect example of gorgeous landscape and a quality calling area. If you cannot go into the thick brush after the bear, have the bears come to you! Call them out!

as easy as possible for a bear to come to you. The same can be said for coyote calling. So, try to position yourself so the bear doesn't have to pass anything major (such as a river) and doesn't have to come way up a hill or through a big rocky cliff area. Remember, you are posing as a tasty meal, and you want to be as easy to get to as possible. Think of yourself as a bear Happy Meal in a drive-through. You're tasty and easy to get.

A mistake beginning callers often make is assuming they did not call anything in because they didn't see anything. Remember, you will have more failed call sets than those that produce animals, especially when you first start out. This is for several reasons. Number one, just because you didn't see any bears does not mean bears did not come in to the call. They just might have spotted you or smelled you. It is going to happen, even to the experts, so don't take it hard if you don't see anything when you start out.

Think about it, you are trying to call in a bear that has the smelling ability equal to seven times that of a bloodhound. Plus, you're stationary, so all the bear has to do is get downwind under cover, sniff your scent, and slip away unnoticed. After that the bear has been educated; it might now be fully aware not to come into that particular call anymore because it relates the call to the scent of a human. Just like when those pesky small perch strip your hook bare before you get the chance to set the hook on a big one, predators will figure you out before you get the chance to put one down. Our goal while calling is to lessen that percentage a bit through knowledge, calling cadence and volume, wind, an extra set of eyes, and some luck.

Now that you are secure against a tree or whatever it may be and have a clear view of your downwind target, you are ready to start calling. On your way to your stand, try to remain as quiet as possible and watch your wind! If you make loud noise or you snapped a few sticks too many and the like, give it a few minutes before you start your set. This allows for the birds to start chirping again—basically to have the sounds of the surrounding area get back to normal before it went quiet from being interrupted by a human. If you are going to make some noise getting to where you want to call, do not be afraid to use a local animal's call to help cover your sound, for example an elk. I have used cow calls as I have stumbled through the brush to let other animals in the area think it is an elk, not a human. Now, if you don't have elk in your area, this might not work, so try a buck snort, perhaps. Remember, too, while you are blowing on a call, no matter the call, you might call something in, so be prepared for that. I have definitely called in bears with cow calls while elk hunting. You must always be cautious when you are using an animal call.

Initially, start your call set quietly. Meaning you don't want to just start blowing on a call full blast or have your e-caller on full volume. This can cause target animals to get freaked out and leave the area, which is referred to as blowing them out of the area. So, start a little quietly; perhaps there is a bear close by that was not disturbed by your walk into the stand site. This has happened to me more than once. Had I not started to predator call, I would have had no idea I was about sixty yards from a bear.

Bears like a constant noise from the caller. This means the set should continue as frequently as possible, unlike when calling for coyotes. Some people suggest using earplugs because the caller bothers them or their ears ring from the noise. I don't wear earplugs, and if at all possible, my ears are exposed so I can hear as clearly as possible. I don't like heavy fitted hats that cover my ears when I am calling provided the weather is cooperating. I also try not to move, so putting in and pulling out earplugs is not an option for me.

Call for a bit with a lower volume level and slowly work up the volume of the call and the intensity of the distress. If you are using a hand call, cup a hand around the end of the call and lift the hand off the call as you blow into it to simulate a mouth opening. At first in the scenario in your head, the rabbit, fawn, calf, or whatever was caught on a fence or had a busted leg is squealing a bit. This is the sound you are trying to replicate. Now, the pain is worse or a predator has found the animal (in your scenario you are setting up) and is beginning to pick at the animal. The desperation should get increasingly worse and the sounds of the call more dire. Also, remember, a rabbit does not have a full grown man's lungs. They are tiny animals with even smaller lungs, so try to sound like the animal you are imitating even by considering their lung capacity. Blow longer and harder for simulating fawns, calves, or even doe. Watch a few videos online on bears killing deer or moose calves, as this will give you a good example of what to simulate and what you don't want to end up as.

Think of bears behaving like a house cat. Dangle a string in front of a cat and they love it. Keep it up and they keep interested. But if you stop playing with the string for a bit, even a minute, the cat soon gets distracted and loses interest. The same is true for bears (or at least some bears—tricky little buggers). You want to keep calling as much as you can and only take breaks to listen briefly. And when you listen, listen closely to the sounds of nature. Are the birds quiet? Did you hear a twig snap? Bears will often snort or make other guttural noises on the way in—are any of these sounding off? Remember, you will often hear bears before you see them even when you are not calling. Of course, then there are those bears you never hear, too. Man, they can be quiet when they want to be!

A very important tip when predator calling is to pay special attention to any squirrels you have in the area. Don't laugh, I am telling you this works! This is one of my favorite tricks. I know this will not work for some of our readers, but those in the woods of the east and west will have pretty good luck with it. Once I start calling, squirrels will sometimes go nuts (no pun intended) at the sounds I am making. The squirrels that are close to you giving off their warning chatter are not really the ones to pay attention to. They are just sounding off to let others know of the racket going on. But if you hear a squirrel about 100 yards off or even farther out start giving its warning chatter, pay very close attention to this sound.

The squirrel is warning the woods for a reason and warning you unintentionally. Just like when you go out deer hunting and happen to disturb a squirrel, it yells at you to warn any animals in the area. Now that you have started calling, predators might be on the move toward you and cause the squirrels to warn others. So, if one is chatting away at you and you hear another squirrel do the same a few minutes later that sounds closer to you, this is a sign. Whatever the squirrel is warning other animals about is coming closer to you. Watch in the direction from which you are hearing the noise. This has tipped me off on deer, bears, coyotes, and bobs numerous times. I like to call it squirrel radar.

Onc time archery elk hunting, I was sitting on a grassy steep hillside with tall pines. A squirrel was above me a few trees downhill barking at me for, I would guess, an hour. I was quite fed up with it and, by the grace of God, I was granted reprieve. A hawk had caught the squirrel's ADD flickering and noise and swooped in to save my sanity. I could hear the hawk cutting through the air as it closed in, I caught the final squeak of the squirrel as it became lunch, and watched as it was carried away with a smile on my face. But, let us get back to calling!

When you rest, rest for a minute or two at the most and keep calling. Some predator callers will want you to call for at least an hour or more. I call for about an hour and then I go quiet and sit to watch the area for about another fifteen minutes or so. Staying at the call site after you are done calling is important because a bear might have been coming in but was uneasy of the set up. So, once all goes quiet, the bear might consider it safer to come out and check the area, thereby exposing itself for a shot or a stalk.

Stick around for a while, as you never know what you might see. I know of several hunters who have quit calling and sat watching their hunting range only to see a cougar come bouncing into the area. Also, before you get up to leave, give any tree lines a good glassing with your binoculars to look carefully for bears hiding on edges. They are hesitant to the leave the safety of cover for

Photo by Justin Haug.

Bears can come into calls running, walking, sneaking, fully charging, or just plain sitting and watching like this fellow.

good reason. We call this hanging up, which can be very frustrating. I have had bears on numerous occasions hang up in the brush for no apparent reason other than they didn't want to leave it no matter what call I used or anything else I did. They have been as close as ten yards breathing, snorting, and snapping brush . . . just not willing to show themselves. Another reason I love calling, even though they hang up like that sometimes, is that it still really gets the blood pumping. In most of these instances, I want to believe they hung up because they didn't see an animal or movement. It made them uneasy or unsure of what was going on. Just a theory of mine.

If you call and are not having much luck in several areas, try a different call or strategy. Are you using a jack-rabbit distress call? Are they a common animal in the area, or are calf elk more common? Toss in a few coyote howls to make it sound like a pack of hungry dogs are tearing into a fawn, then bleat on a fawn call to sound as desperate and hopeless as possible. This is a pretty good scenario throughout the country, since we have coyotes and deer pretty much everywhere. Again, if you are having trouble trying to figure out what an animal in distress would sound like, look up a video on YouTube. I prefer to actually watch or listen to animals that are really being attacked to try to replicate those sounds. You can find some videos of black bears taking out deer and moose calves, among other things. I would like to record my La Mancha goats when they are freaked out. I am sure they would call something in with their distress. Perhaps once I figure out how to do that, it will be my ace in the hole call—something no one else is using.

If everyone and their mother uses the same old rabbit distress calling in your hunting area, change calls to something oddball, such as a pig squealer or even a cub distress. Be careful with cub distress calls, as you are likely to get a sow bear who is none too happy coming into it. Try to give yourself the best edge possible. Do you have a power-line cut or gas-line cut with timber on either side or a clear-cut area? Pick yourself up a decoy of some sort to add to your call set. Montana Decoys makes some photorealistic decoys of fawns, cow elk, and so on that are light and affordable. This could be the visual difference that you need to get that bear to break loose.

Let's stop and ponder that for a minute. You are making all sorts of noise of a supposed dying animal. Other than the sound, is there any other evidence for the predator to believe there is something going on? Any movement? Most animals, when they are in their death throes, are twisting and

Here is Fawnzy by Montana Decoy. A great addition to any predator caller, this is a photorealistic way to add sight as an attractant for predators, specifically bears. In this picture, you will also notice I have placed the FOXPRO Inferno with the FoxJack 2 attachment slightly hidden in the grass. The combo of both the Fawnzy and the motion and sound put out by the Inferno and FoxJack 2 attachment is an absolutely lethal combination. I have the Inferno placed strategically so the FoxJack 2 movement will be close to the Fawnzy's tail end with the idea that the movement will cause the bear to think it is the flicking of the fawn's tail. The Fawnzy is lightweight and easy to assemble for transport.

going nuts, moving brush, and creating lots of movement. So, a decoy that supplies some sort of visual is very helpful. I have even seen a picture of a bear that bit right down on a decoy of a fawn. It was pretty amazing. I have personally had hawks take out my Mojo Critter and fly off with a piece of it. I have almost lost my hat to birds of prey I don't know how many times. I have literally ducked as hawks have come in to check me out.

Weather and terrain, no question, will affect your calling. A strong wind will reduce your ability to get sound out far. A heavily timbered area will impede your calls, whereas a wide-open, lightly timbered sage flat will allow your sound to carry pretty far. Rain will also keep your sound muffled. A crisp, clear, cold morning will no doubt let your call carry for some distance. Keep weather and terrain in consideration when choosing when and where to call. Be prepared to change up your routine to match the conditions. Would you use a floating frog for bass in the middle of a deep lake on a windy day? Probably not, since they are normally used in the shallows on calm days. The same goes for calling. You must adapt and will, therefore, overcome.

I rarely call in heavy wind or rain, as there just doesn't seem to be much point. If there is a medium to strong wind, I prefer to keep the wind in my face and travel my hunting area glassing for bears eating or looking for bears traveling from one spot to another. I will save the calling for another day. The wind and rain will help cover my scent and sound but will not do my calling much good, so I change my tactics to match my conditions. Try to pick light wind days for best results with calling. If it is hot out, pick a watering hole or creek to call by, as this is again using the weather to help you increase your chance of success. Bears will often take midday naps by food sources or water sources. Of course, so will the bear hunter. I think that is half the reason I love bear hunting so much, is taking a midday nap after eating some sun-warmed blackberries is half the reason I love bear hunting so much. You know, bears really have the life.

I recently went to Alaska for a black bear hunt. It was my first time to the great state, and what a state it is. I absolutely loved it. However, my time was very short. My childhood buddy and photographer of many shots in this book, Justin Haug, called me up one summer afternoon and invited me to Alaska for a black bear hunt with the only cost being that of an out of state bear tag, hunting license, locking tag, and flight. How could I say no? Plus the wife gave me permission, so off I went for a whirlwind of a trip—literally I had a day and a morning to hunt during the four-day trip. I bring this up for a reason about wind.

I am going to keep this a bit short but will tell the extended version of the story in the Personal Calling Stories chapter. During my first day that I was able to hunt (I was unable to hunt the first day I arrived into the bush, as I was flown into the area), the wind had picked up quite a bit and was blowing off a gorgeous glacial valley. I was set in a swampy flat facing an enormous mountainside with brush that covered the first two thirds of the mountain, and the brush reached well over my head. There were some occasional openings in which I could spot an animal if it came out.

With the wind howling and Justin by my side with his trusty camera, we decided to give calling a try even though it was windy and not ideal. My reasoning was that it was so brushy and had poured the night before, so I had no desire to stumble through twelve-foot alders and willows searching for a bear that would hear me several hundred yards before I got to it. My only hope in this situation was trying to spot something in the openings or calling into the brush hoping to break something loose.

We set up on a rock outcropping outside of our camp, and I placed the FOXPRO Inferno about sixty yards from my position with the FoxJack 2 attached to it. A creek bottom ran out off the mountain in front of us choked with brush and the remains of dying salmon carrying on their last effort for the circle of life. I turned it up to about volume eighteen out of twenty because I knew how loud it was with the wind cutting through the brush. Justin was tucked into the brush just above me to my right. Not five minutes into the call session (the timer on the FOXPRO remote confirmed this), a bear popped out about 500 yards from our position into one of the clear spots I was mentioning. Not only was this exciting for me as always, but Justin had not really experienced anything like this before, so he was happy to be able to get some shots of the bear as it sat down and contemplated what the racket was and if it was worth investigating. Even in heavy wind, surrounded by thick brush, and at a pretty good distance, that bear heard the distress calls coming from

Photo courtesy of Justin Haug.

Called in close with the FOXPRO Inferno and FoxJack 2 attachment (just out of the picture), you couldn't have asked for more from an e-caller. If only it had been a boar! Outstanding product. Notice how wet the bears are? They came out of super thick brush with the wind howling and rain just letting up. This is a testament to the Inferno's ability to cut through ambient noise and get the bears to come to you.

the FOXPRO and came out of the otherwise gnarled mess of brush to let me know bears were close by. She later came down to within about forty yards of my position with her gorgeous three cubs. What a good momma she was. As soon as she smelled us, she was out of there. I was just getting ready to let her know she was getting too close (I was above her on the rock outcropping, remember) when she decided that was enough.

My point is twofold here. One, even in heavy wind, calling can give you an excellent advantage in an otherwise difficult situation to hunt. Trying to get close to a bear in that mess quietly, while possible, would be painstakingly difficult, so why not have the bear come to us? My second point was confirmed by the momma. It took her forty-five to fifty minutes to get down to the call. She was stuck with three little ones in tow, who would have rather played on a rock cliff for a while than find what momma was trying to eat. Bears will take their time coming into calls when they feel like it. They are not always like a coyote coming into a call by fifteen minutes or a half hour. It takes patience and persistence when calling bears. There is much more to this tale, but we will get to that in a bit. As she ran off, I was again so thankful to be able to share that moment with the bear, the cubs, and my friend. There I was in the wilds of Alaska with nobody around for miles, and I was able to experience such a wonderful moment. It was another hunting moment that will last me forever.

Now, we all make mistakes, especially when we are new at something. I certainly have made mine when it comes to calling, but I have tried to learn from them as best I can. I will discuss more of this later in the book, but for now let me touch on a few of the common mistakes made when calling.

When I first started out calling, I thought I needed to keep the wind in my face and have that as my main shooting lane. It wasn't until I watched some good coyote videos by Randy Anderson that I learned how predators will circle you while trying to smell you out. I was facing the wrong direction on several sets; Lord knows how many animals I educated. So, I learned to have my shooting lane downwind. Follow that rule first and foremost. A crosswind isn't so bad either. You just have to adjust your shooting lane to match the wind.

I would get discouraged calling if something didn't show up, but I have been called stubborn more than once, especially by my wife, so I kept trying at it. Do not get discouraged and give up when set after set you do not see anything. Remember, it is like fishing, you will have your good fishing days and bad ones. Let us not forget the saying, "A bad day fishing beats a good day working." I have that sign above my door in my man cave. I should have one that replaces "fishing" with "calling." The point here is to keep casting out, keep calling, and you will get a bite sooner or later. You just have to find out what they are biting on. Well, I guess it is okay to get discouraged when calling, as I still do sometimes, just don't give up on it. Calling is an amazing tool that any bear hunter can utilize. It is by far one of the most exciting hunting strategies I have ever used.

Avoid strong smelling foods before calling. For example, don't chew gum, avoid smoking, and maybe don't eat fish or garlic right before going out. While I am not a subscriber to the whole carbon clothes and scent spray craze, I do try a few things to keep my scent down. Try not to hustle and sweat when you are headed to your hunting or calling area. Keeping your sweat level down will not only reduce your scent, but also you will be walking slower, and you never know, you might observe a bear before you ever get to your calling spot. Be mindful of your scent. Be mindful of touching your electronic caller or decoy with your bare hands. Try to touch them with gloves on so as to not leave as much human scent. Or be like one of my elk hunting buddies named Art and drink coffee and smoke while sitting on a stump and the animals will come right to you. I think every hunter has a friend like that—you know what I am talking about.

Do not stick to the same old call. How does the saying go? "The definition of insanity is doing the same thing over and over and expecting a different result," or something like that. If you are not having luck with one type of call, try a different call with a different tempo or volume. Change up your set, add a decoy, if legal, or use some scents or attractants (again, check your regulations before this). Change can be good. Especially when you are predator calling. A combo of a decoy with movement and calling can be deadly. I used a snowshoe hare distress in one of my sets in Alaska with some interest. I changed it to jackrabbit distress, and they really got moving in. Why? Perhaps it was a different sound than they normally hear, I am not sure, but I know changing it up worked.

Remember, you are trying to make the most realistic scenario possible to fool an animal that is more powerful than you, can out-smell you, knows the land, and knows how to move like a ghost. If you cannot afford a decoy, grab some thin fishing line and tie it to a bush out about ten feet or so in front of you. Tug on it slightly as you call, causing the bush to move. It will add the movement you might need. I have used this technique a little bit here and there. It does work, but you have to try to hide the movement of your hands. If you do use this, be sure to pick up the fishing line after you are done. Pack in, pack out.

I touched on it earlier, but once you finish your set (when you are all done calling), don't just get up and walk off. Stick around for a little bit—even five minutes or so. You never know what might come in. Also, as you end your set in the scenario you have set up, whatever has been screaming is now dying, so have it sound that way. Your calling should be getting weaker and weaker near the end until you finally go quiet. Remember, you are mimicking a dying animal that is likely caught by a fence or being ripped apart by another predator. Try to make it sound that way; be convincing. Don't just randomly blow on the call with no emotion or heart in it. Be desperate sounding, exhausted, whiny, and basically dying. Presentation of the sound can go a long way for your set. Build a scenario and stick to it to the end. Change the scenario up for the next

This prime furred coyote came into one of my sets, and I was happy to do my part and put him on the man cave wall. Save a fawn, pop a coyote. Remember, it is not just bears that come into predator calls but also cougars, coyotes, bobcat, deer, elk, grizzlies, and, yes, even other hunters.

call session if you didn't have much luck on the previous scenario. Find what works.

Again, now that the calling is done, sit quietly despite how bad your knees and butt are yelling at you to stand up. Yes, I know the feeling; even though as I write this I am still young, twenty-some years in construction can take a toll on a fellow's body. Wait, watch, listen, and glass slowly. Sit for fifteen minutes or so depending on how you feel and how the situation feels to you. If all else fails and nothing shows up, you can circle the area to see if any tracks reveal themselves. I have often found tracks of animals I believe came into a call and failed to reveal themselves. Remember, just because you didn't see an animal come in does not mean one did not. Finding tracks can help you from being too discouraged. It gives some hope that you actually did call something in.

Off to the next set; move to the next good looking spot. This can be a few miles away or less than 1000 yards depending on terrain. Giving yourself time to do a few sets will increase your experience in calling and help build on your past situations. If you are hunting with a partner, have them call this time around so you can take a break and remain focused on the hunt. Remember to set up where you can see things, up high if you can, with clear shooting lanes, and watch that wind!

I usually bring five calls or so with me when I go out. Not that I use them all in one set, but I have the option to use them in that set or others. Or if my call gets clogged or frozen, I can switch to another. Give yourself options. You will likely find a call that you have good luck with or just plain like the sound of. I know I have a few that way. Some calls will get a bit full of spit after calling for an hour or so. Know how to take your call apart if you can so you can dry and clean it. Some closed- and open-reed calls you can take apart, but others are one piece. Get to know your equipment before you head out so you can deal with changing conditions.

Windy conditions are not the only ones I like to avoid. Fog is another. It limits your field of view and therefore your range. I recently took my stepson out calling for bears on a foggy day. It was a day he had off from school and I, too, from work, so it worked out. Granted, the weather didn't cooperate, but that's okay. We went anyway. On the way to the set area, we came upon some fresh cougar scat and tracks. As young boys do, he was checking out the scat, asking what it was from, how fresh it was, and so on.

We found a log landing that we could tuck ourselves into as the fog swirled around us. It was dead quiet out, as there was no wind at the time. We started to call even though my stepson Haydin was busy trying *not* to kick a spider that was by his foot. You can't blame a kid of eleven for not holding still all the time. It was a miracle any of my uncles didn't ditch me in the woods at that age, since I am sure I sounded like a bulldozer stumbling through clear-cuts. Regardless of his movement and our lack of seeing anything, I think we did have some success.

If you find bear sign of any sort, you might want to consider calling and finding out if the bear is still hanging around. I found this bear hair on a sapling after the bear had marked its territory. If you find hair, this is usually a good sign. Bear hair will not stay on thorns or branches forever. This usually indicates a fairly fresh sign. This is less true about deer or elk hair, which is rubbed heavily on trees with pitch, which causes it to stick in place.

Squirrels had started their warning calls some distance away. As the set progressed, the warning calls became closer and closer until about sixty yards out they stopped coming in. Was it the cougar whose scat we saw? A bear or coyote? I would place money on a cat, as whatever it was

was extremely quiet and cautious. We never did see it. As we gave up and headed back to the truck, we were lucky enough to be able to bag a grouse, which we later had for dinner. My point here? Yes, it was foggy and not ideal, but the boy and I got to share some great times outdoors together. We never would have gotten that grouse if we just stayed inside. And my stepson never would have been able to learn how to tell a cat track from a dog track or see the fresh cougar scat. Call when you can, and spend time with your loved ones. Tomorrow isn't guaranteed.

Also remember when you call that we all have different likes and dislikes when it comes to how we hunt. Some prefer using tree stands instead of spot and stalk, some like archery, and others prefer modern firearms. Find what you like about calling, and you will have more success, I feel. If you like what you are doing, success comes easier. If you like closed-reed calls, keep at it. If you feel safer with electronic calls or you feel you can stay hidden better using that style of call, go with that. Calling for bears is not brain surgery, but there are certainly tricks of the trade. Your best research for calling is the research you do on your own out in the field. Just be safe with it and have fun, as it is one heck of a pastime!

The time of year can make a big difference in your calling success, too. If it is midsummer and there are lots of berries around or other food sources, calling might not be as effective as it is in the spring or late fall. Why is that, you ask? Food is readily available, and a bear can be hesitant to leave a tasty berry bush for the promise of something making lots of noise. I have seen it happen firsthand. I called in a bear over a ridgetop, and the bear decided to come check me out; halfway down the hill, boom—he noticed a nice huckleberry bush and decided this was better than what I was offering!

This is not to say a bear will not show up when you call in the summer—it just might not work as well as it does at other times. That should not, however, stop you from calling into a thick, nasty pile of brush or tree line that you think might contain bears. You could very well bust a bear loose and get it to show itself, so give it a shot. I know I always do.

As I write this, snow is beginning to fall in the foothills around me; it's November 9. We are expecting about eighteen inches of snow in some of our mountain passes this week. This weekend is the final weekend for bear hunting in my home state. You can bet I am going out to try my hand at calling this weekend despite the weather, which is forecasting rain and wind. I am hoping to work my way up high in elevation. Bears are finishing up their food gathering, and a nice wounded animal would make a great topper for a hungry bear's meal. Late-season calling can be very productive if you can just find where the bears will be hanging out. Not to mention, it's prime hide time. Thick, warm, amazing hides are on bears and are wonderful trophies for any successful hunter.

Calling is not foolproof—it has its time and place. It does add to the arsenal of the black-bear hunter. Don't hesitate to add it to your arsenal, as well.

Chapter Six

Personal Calling Stories

The following are true accounts of my personal experiences calling bears. I wanted to include these stories in the book for a couple of reasons. For one, I wanted to let you know what you can expect when calling, especially if you have never called bears before. If these stories freak you out, well, that's good. That means you might take some necessary precautions when you call, which I would highly recommend.

Second, I think some of them are entertaining enough that you might find they are noteworthy. I have had success and failure in calling, and these are my prime examples. With that said, here are some of my more entertaining follies while bear calling. Enjoy!

THE TALE FROM ALASKA, "HUNGER COUNTRY"

I spoke briefly of this story earlier in the book. It is about the momma sow and her three cubs that came into the FOXPRO Inferno—but let me expand on the full story. As previously stated, I was invited for a whirlwind trip with a lifelong friend of mine, Justin Haug. You might notice his name associated with many of the photographs in this book. We have known each other since kindergarten and have hunted off and on through the years. Basically, I would have a total of about one full day and a morning to hunt a unit that normally has about a 15 percent success rate for out-of-state black-bear hunters, according to the Alaska Fish and Game regulations. When I was reading up on the Alaska game rules, I checked the success rates, and I knew this was going to be a challenge. I just hoped I was up for it.

I arrived in Anchorage, and Justin and his Marine brother, Joel, picked me up from the airport. We soon met my other friend, who was going to fly us into the area. The wind was picking up, and we were not sure if we were going to be able to make it into the hunting area. My first trip in a Super Cub airplane was kind of scary but amazing nonetheless. If you have never ridden in one, think of a tandem bike with wings. As the pilot and I bounced along above a huge glacier, he pointed out different points of interest. It was getting pretty windy, so he asked where I wanted to be dropped off. I said, "Anywhere looks as good as anyplace else!" The hunting area we chose was basically the nearest landing strip he knew of—and down we went. The wind was picking up, and judging from the dark clouds that crowned the sky above the glacier, I was in for an interesting late afternoon and evening.

As we unloaded my gear onto the very short runway that was lined by scrub brush and tucked into an enormous valley, the pilot asked, "Are you good?"

"I am," I replied—reassuring him and me—and he said he would see me in an hour or so, hopefully. That is, if the wind didn't ground him from bringing back Justin. If that happened, I was on my own. Justin was not hunting this trip but wanted to tag along so he could take pictures of the hunt. I was happy to be with him not only for safety but for company, as well. Off he went, and I was alone. Very alone. But this was not the first time I had been that way in the woods. It was, however, the first time I had been to Alaska and alone, so that was briefly unnerving. I was not sure what to expect. I had my pistol at my side and loaded my rifle for safety.

I quickly set up my tent to keep my gear dry if it started to rain, which looked likely. By the time I got all set up, the plane came back with Justin. We unloaded his gear, and the pilot headed off back home. We set up camp and started glassing.

Now, let me describe what we were looking at. To the east and west of camp, we had massive ancient glaciers on either side of the valley. The western glacier was more visible from our camp and had shale slides that lined parts of the edges (glacial till, I believe it is called) about a mile away from camp. We were set up by some large rocks, about thirty feet tall or so, that had some alders and willows surrounding them. Thankfully, we were able to use the rocks to block the wind. The wind picked up some and was cutting through the mountain valley without anything stopping it. To the north and south were glorious mountainsides that towered far above us. I am from Washington, so I am used to mountains. But these mountains were awe-inspiring. Truly amazing. At the base of the mountains were willows and other tall, foreboding brush of all sorts. About two thirds of the way up the mountainsides, the brush gave way to what appeared to be vast blueberry fields, all changing colors of red and yellow.

Undoubtedly this was God's country.

As I looked around at the scenery, I gave thanks to the Lord, for however brief my visit was to this valley and no matter the outcome of the hunt, I knew I was already successful just to be there at that moment. It didn't matter if I took a bear; what really mattered to me was our safety and general fellowship. It is a rarity that I get to spend time with Justin anymore, as we live on opposite sides of the state, and even rarer when I am in Alaska. I just took a breath and let it all sink into my soul.

I laid my dad's Mystery Ranch backpack up against a rock by my tent, plopped down, and started to glass with my Leupold binoculars. Per Alaska hunting regulations, you are not allowed to hunt black bear the same day you fly, so the next day would be my first day of hunting, which was fine by me. I just wanted to kick back and enjoy the sights after flying from Seattle to this amazing valley. It was a few hours until dark, and it didn't take us long to find our first bear. He was along the shale, which bordered one of the glaciers, and looked like an absolute tank of a bear. From that distance, that black blob looked like a bruiser. He was plodding along the shale and would occasionally stop to dig. He was digging for pika, and I got to watch him. It was a great treat to observe the bear's actions, and it got my hopes up for the next day. He had a swagger that looked like he owned the place. He probably did.

I glassed a bit more and much closer to camp, and there was another bear! He was crawling along a nasty rock face and eating what I believed to be red berries off some tree, but I could not be sure at that distance. The bear reminded me of, well, *me* one time when I was hunting. He looked like he was wondering how he got there and how he was going to get down. Sometimes you travel along a steep embankment and can't go forward, and once you look back you're not sure how you got there in the first place. I am sure he was well prepared and not worried, however. As I watched him, I glassed a bit farther away, and another bear popped out between that bear on the cliff and the bear digging for pika. Three bears, all well within hiking distance. I told Justin that this looked promising. He agreed.

Darkness arrived, we built a fire, and we settled down for some mountain house freeze-dried meals. Looking at the terrain, I explained there was no way I was going to bust brush looking for bears in that soaking mess. Rather, I was going to call them to me. Justin agreed but had never experienced bear calling before. He was in for a treat. Calling was really the only logical thing to do in this situation, in my opinion. Plus, it would make for a thrilling day!

That night, I was restless. I was a bit unnerved about sleeping out there alone in a very confined tent. Don't get me wrong, I have slept outside much of my life alone, hunting, and so forth. This was just new territory for me. Plus, I think I was a bit anxious for the morning hunt. The rain pounded the tents that night, but the rock formations we were butted up against shielded us from the worst of the glacial wind, thankfully. I woke up throughout the night from my own snores (half thinking it was a bear) and hoping that the tent would last through the nasty storm, which it did.

In the morning, I awoke to scattered clouds and the breaking sun. Once I coaxed Justin out of bed with the promise of a nice morning weather-wise, conditions changed to a light rain, and we donned our rain gear. We headed a few hundred yards away from camp to gather up water from a stream that rolled off the mountainside and poured into a larger creek that eventually fed into a web of beaver ponds and tributaries. I was explaining how my Steripen (a water purifier that uses light to kill bacteria and protozoa) worked when we heard some rustling in the willows on the other side of the creek. I quickly grabbed my Tikka .300 WSM and lip squeaked in an attempt to coax out whatever was in there. Nothing showed up. After gathering our water, we headed back to camp and cooked a little breakfast.

A side note here—always make sure to purify your water. This is a basic hunter's skill, but you definitely do not want to drink contaminated water and have to deal with the stomach ailments that will plague you. If you have no other option, you can always boil your water to kill any nasty bacteria and ensure it is safe to drink. Remember, fast, free-flowing water is best. Avoid swampy, stagnant water if at all possible.

I decided there was not much reason to travel too far, as we were right by a nice place to call. We walked a bit outside of camp (100 yards or so) and climbed on top of the biggest rock formation that overlooked the hillside. This would allow us to view a few openings in the brush on the

This is a photo of the creek we drank out of not far from our drop camp. Make sure to always clean your water before drinking it with a filter or by boiling. Sure beats bottled water.

hillside closest to us (400 to 500 yards or so), as well as give us some safety being up in the rocks and, finally, give us a nice view of the valley floor, which we were camping on.

I set up the FOXPRO Inferno about sixty yards to the left (downwind side) of where my shooting position was going to be. The e-caller also had the FoxJack 2 on it as a motion decoy. I started up with a snowshoe hare distress on a high volume level. The wind was howling right to left, a nice crosswind. My concern was that it was going to be so noisy in the brush due to the wind that the e-caller would not be able to penetrate and get to the bears. I was wrong. Not five minutes into the set, a bear came out of the brush at about 500 yards and sat down looking right at us. I called out to Justin that there was a bear. He was looking slightly off to the left down the valley and readjusted to get shots of the bear sitting.

While my excitement was increasing, my hopes of a shot disappeared when two cubs showed up right by momma. I didn't mind so much; I absolutely love watching bears, and a sow with cubs is a special treat. They wandered about in the opening, as the mother was still trying to figure out if it was worthwhile to check out all noise from below. I then heard a nasty cry coming from just uphill of the sow. She bolted toward the cry, and I recognized it as a cub bawl. He must have gotten separated but quickly rejoined the party. I decided to change from a snowshoe hare

Photo courtesy of Justin Haug.

This bear came right out of the brush within minutes of turning on the FOXPRO Inferno and FoxJack 2 motion decoy. Those products work, and this is proof!

distress to a jackrabbit distress, and sure enough, she committed to coming down—however, ever so slowly. So, now the sow was on the way with three cubs in tow. What a good momma! I happened to glance to my right and spotted a coyote running as fast as his legs could carry him, but he was straining to lift a whole dead salmon as he ran. He cut across the valley floor dodging pockets of brush and bounding through little fingers of the creek. I mouth called to him, and he paused to look back but decided he had enough food at the moment and carried on. I've never seen a coyote carry a spawned-out salmon before—pretty cool!

On her way down, the momma headed into the brush, and we lost sight of her for a while. The call was still running at about volume eighteen out of twenty. I increased to twenty when we lost sight of her to keep her interested. Ten minutes or so later, she popped out much closer to the valley floor. I don't think she ever lost interest, but I wanted to make sure we kept her coming. Nevertheless, the rambunctious cubs decided to hang out on a rocky cliff and come down that way. The mom, you could tell, was none too pleased but waited patiently for the cubs to catch up near the bottom of the rocks. They were then about 300 yards away and on the valley floor. I quickly lost sight of the bears in the brush again.

This is a view from where I called the bear in. Note that I am up high and have a decent view for safety, which is something you must consider, especially when predator calling in grizzly-bear country.

You could catch glimpses of her as she came closer. Walking in, you could see her nose working the air for the scent of whatever was making that noise, her mouth opening and closing as she sucked in air with her nose. She was downwind of me, as bears like to be. By now, I had shut off the volume of the caller, but the bear still tuned into the area where the sound was coming from and headed right for it. The cubs followed along completely unaware of their mission. She walked through the brush and was now in the wide open under 100 yards. In the state of Alaska, it is illegal to shoot a sow with cubs—not to mention, this is not something I would knowingly do, anyway. I love bears and want them to continue to succeed and flourish; again, it was such a treat to be able to watch all of this unfold. The avoidance of shooting a sow with a cub is a great point of relevance in defense of those who bait bears.

She got to within a few feet of the caller, and I whispered to Justin that I was going to stand up and let her know I was there. I could hear Justin's camera click away. As soon as I said that, she winded us anyway and jogged away to my right into some willows and then headed back up the hill. One cub decided to hang back and smell something on the ground but quickly realized he was being left and ran to catch up. Momma and cubs went along safely, we had a successful calling session with pictures—what more could we have asked for? As she left, we chatted about how cool that was, how interesting it was to be able to watch the bear wonder what the noise was, and how cute those cubs were. What a great start.

We then decided to try to cut across the valley floor to where that tank of a bear was digging up pika or marmots the night before. We ended up doing a big circle, as we did not have the right boots to cross what we were going to have to cross. It reminded me of the dead marshes from *Lord of the Rings: The Two Towers* movie. Except moose tracks covered much of the area instead of Nazgul. Yes, I am a nerd. I accept it. So, trying to get to the shale seemed to be a bust. We decided to follow the footing of the hill on the valley floor and call here and there as we went.

It was a nice hike, but we didn't have much calling success. The wind had picked up substantially, and it was a bit disheartening to have the weather against us for such a short hunt. Undeterred, we continued on and hiked to a knob that overlooked a massive glacier feeding into a huge lake dotted with icebergs. The remains of a float plane on the brushy knob sat as a reminder that not everyone makes it out of the bush alive. Looking down onto the valley floor was difficult. If you looked in the direction of the wind, it was blowing so fast and cold that your eyes would water. We stayed for a bit and decided to head back toward camp for a late lunch.

We had lunch of beef Stroganoff and noticed not too far from where the cliff-hanging bear was the previous night, there was another marauding bear looking to pack on a few more pounds on this mid-September day. We decided to make a break for it and try to call the bear if we could get within range. We had traveled toward the bear's area earlier in the day, so we knew how to get there quickly through the swamp. After getting within a few hundred yards of where I believed the bear to be, I set up the FOXPRO Inferno to call. It was not an ideal calling situation because there were tall trees and brush between us and the bear, and we were below the bear. This meant the sound would have to cut through those trees to get to the bear. In addition, and unknown to me until I got into position, we had a loud creek flowing between us, which was a greater hindrance for having the sound carry. We set up, tucked into some brush with a beaver pond to our backs, and called for about an hour with no visible luck. I truly believe this was in part due to the fact that the bear didn't hear us. The wind was still blowing but calming down, the creek was loud, and we had a good amount of physical barriers between us. But, you cannot win them all, so we packed up and worked our way back to camp to plan our next attack.

After getting back to camp, my plan was to sit and glass with the hope of spotting a bear close enough to make a move on it. It was getting to be late afternoon. No sooner had I set down my pack than Justin said, "There's a bear!" Sure enough, right where that sow had come out of the brush in the morning was a bear working its way along the opening eating berries.

I quickly tossed my pack back on, and we hustled to the same rock formation right outside of camp 100 yards or so away. We quickly climbed the slick rock, and I got set up. Justin tucked into the brush behind me with his camera. The wind had died down, but we still had about a ten-mile-an-hour crosswind from right to left. The bear was getting ready to disappear into the brush, so I quickly grabbed my mouth call and squealed loudly on it, frantically. Really, I was a bit frantic. I didn't want the bear to disappear, and I wanted some more action!

The bear plopped right down, sat, and watched and listened for a few minutes—then committed. He headed right down the hill into the brush— right for us. Not two minutes later, another bear popped out from above where the first bear

When you have a bear charging in at you from less than 100 yards (plus two more barreling downhill at you), your heart really starts to pump! This is the bear I shot as she was running in to us. At this point she was barely thirty yards away. Notice how focused her eyes are, not toward the photographer, but toward what was making all the noise—me. She has iced her stare off to her right, which is where I was when this photo was taken.

Photo by Justin Haug.

was, and now he was on his way down. I turned to Justin and said, "Two bears are coming in!" As I turned my head to the right to tell Justin this, I saw a fox running on the valley floor away from us and another bear coming right for us at under 100 yards! The fox had seen that bear and was not hanging around for any of this. "Three bears, there is one right there, can you see it!" I exclaimed. He was unable to see the closest bear because of the brush in front of him. The bear who was running at us at under 100 yards was flanking a patch of willows we had in front of the rock we were sitting on. She slowed her pace and stopped while rethinking the situation. She decided to try and wind us. Again, that is key—they like to head downwind, so watch your downwind side. I continued to blast on the mouth call, and she continued to look toward me, her eyes cutting right through me.

As she backtracked to go around the willows and try to wind us, she crossed directly in front of us but was protected by the yellow willows and brush. Keep in mind, I still had two other bears barreling down the hill at us. As she worked her way closer, her pace picked up. I did not see any cubs with her at any point, which was a good thing. She made it all the way around the willows and was about fifteen yards from where, earlier in the day, nature had called to me. She was at maybe thirty yards. I heard Justin's camera shutters blasting away as I aimed

Photo by Justin Haug.

You know the saying, hunting is all fun and games until you shoot something, then the work begins. Here I am breaking out my Havalon Hydra double knife. Notice my rifle, the Mule, sitting pretty on the bipod out of the dirt.

for her head. I didn't really have a good broadside shot or angle, so I decided to take a head shot. I let my .300 WSM (the Mule) kick, and the bear piled right up in her tracks; she never saw it coming. It was kind of shock after that for the both of us—how quickly it changed from settling down at camp to having three bears barreling into our calls in a matter of minutes. We climbed down off the rock well aware that the other two bears we saw might still be on the way and there could be more we did not see.

We dragged the bear away from the standing brush, more out in the open to avoid any surprises, and I got to work on field dressing the bear after notching my tag and attaching the locking metal tag as required. What an amazing day of calling. We were able to finish up field dressing right at dark thanks to the amazingly sharp Havalon Hydra double knife. That double knife and bone-saw combo was all I needed to gut, bone, and skin that bear, which is rare. Justin actually said, "I don't know what is scarier, you calling in those bears or watching you use that razor-sharp knife!" Not that I was being unsafe, but he could see how sharp it was, and he didn't want me to filet myself since we were a bit out of range of a hospital. We hung the meat as best we could and tucked into bed that night. That morning, I spotted three more bears in the same area before flying out on the bush plane

In this picture, you will notice the new Havalon Hydra, the only knife I needed to clean, bone, and skin this entire bear. Amazingly sharp and extremely lightweight, the Havalon Hydra has been the only knife I needed for two bears and a deer in the season of 2015.

There are several impressions I want you to gather from this story. Bears can hear you call pretty well even in blustery conditions. I also want to point out how differently the bears came into the calls. The momma came in, but it took her about forty-five minutes or so. The other two just started walking quickly down the hill toward us, and the one I shot was running full bore until she got close, when she slowed down only briefly. These are all great examples of how bears *might* come in. They are also all examples of why you must be on your toes when you call predators. We were lucky we didn't have a bear come up on the other side of the rock formation we were sitting on, which could have easily happened, for sure.

She was a dry sow, five feet, seven inches nose to tail with decaying teeth and missing some claws from her front paw, which was curious to see. I would have loved to know the story behind that situation. So, the bear hunting gods were really shining on me that day. That trip, I could not have asked for a better hunt, everything worked out perfect, and with good company, too. That usually never happens in hunting, as I am sure most of you are well aware. Would I have liked to go after that big boar I saw the first night? Yes. If I had more time on the trip, I am sure I would have held out for a bigger bear; but, in this case, I was not about to look a gift horse in the mouth. A coworker of mine called the area I was hunting "hunger country." I rather like the term. Although the bear had plenty of berries, dead salmon, and, from what I could tell, moose to harass, it still looked to be a tough place to make a living for just about anything that called it home. I have nothing but love and admiration for black bears.

Photo by Justin Haug.

The charging sow and me—a glorious end to a whirlwind of a trip.

Every animal has a story to tell, and this sow was no different. I wonder how she lost her claws. The local biologist thought perhaps a trap, but my local friend and pilot said no one really traps up there. Who knows?!

UNCONVENTIONAL CALLING

In this brief example, I was not targeting bears, but I was still using a call to attract animals. I was elk hunting with my bow in eastern Washington at the time. I always see hunting shows on which elk hunters are using big bugle calls, trying to sound all massive, and making it a perfect sounding bugle, and I am sure they do work. I am not an elk specialist, although I think I am no slouch, either. Personally, I think sounding like a small scrapper elk waiting to get his butt kicked sounds better to bigger elk and brings in bulls the same if not better than massive bugles. I reached this conclusion because I have called in lots of bull elk just using my open-reed coyote howler, which definitely does not sound like a massive bull. How I was led to try out this method is simple. I was hunting along a deep ravine, when on the other side of the ravine I saw a bull elk racking his antlers all over a poor helpless pine. I do not own a big bugle call, and all I had was my coyote howler. So, I tried to make it sound like a bull elk bugling, kind of long and deep and a bit throaty. It caught the elk's attention instantly, and he bugled back and thrashed his antlers some more.

After a few bugles back and forth, the elk committed to coming in, and he trotted his way the 600 yards or so all the way across the gulley. Eventually, he got within about fifteen yards before I said, "Boo!" and scared him off. My very basic point in this story is unconventional calling can work and work well. I now only use my coyote howler for elk bugles (I do not carry a standard elk bugle), and my brother John has caught on to that strategy. Don't think you have to be like the rest of the people hunting your quarry, as far as calling is concerned. Try different sounds the animal has not heard. Try to think like a bear—you basically just want to pique the bear's interest enough so it will commit and come to the call. I have called in bears using nothing more than my coyote howler sounding like a pup in distress. I have seen bears charge at this sound. I guess a tasty coyote pup is on a bear's menu, when available. Remember, use what you have available, and be creative with it. Try to mimic the family goat on a deer bleat call, whimper like a dog on a coyote call, and so on. Hunting in an area that doesn't have jackrabbits? Try a jackrabbit distress call for the simple fact that the bears might not have heard that sound before and wonder what it is.

CURIOUS CUB AND MOMMA BEAR

I remember this story quite well, as it was one of the first times I had successfully called in a bear. I had arrived on the foothills of the Snoqualmie Pass of Washington, which, at the time, was a mere thirty-minute drive from my house on Lake Sammamish—that is, if traffic didn't get in the way. I parked at the gate, which was just off a main highway where people, most of them completely unaware, drive right by a black-bear hunting gold mine on their way to work. I loaded up my backpack, my trusty .45 caliber Glock, and my Tikka .300 WSM, affectionately known as the Mule due to its kick.

I crossed the beaver pond and began my trek uphill along the old gravel logging road to a spot where I loved to call. It overlooked a wonderful sloped area, which remained cleared for the power lines that towered overhead and fed the various surrounding cities. My brother David was kind enough to show me this area. I decided to cut through what I have come to call Mosquito Alley, an older logging road that was named due to its nasty biting inhabitants. They typically sped up my pace as I slinked my way down the shortcut. I spotted the occasional blackberry bush that had been ripped by a bear, the leaves slowly going brown from the assault. I got to the end of the road that connects to another side road, which in turn connects to the main road.

I glanced up the hill and noticed a bull elk and some cows rummaging around about where I wanted to call from. They slowly worked their way into the tall trees, and I decided to head on up, as I was not seeing any bears (more importantly, not hearing any) close by. As I hiked farther up the hill so I could look downhill and have a clear shot of the clearings, I blissfully munched on the sun-warmed blackberries and luscious red huckleberries. What is not to like about bear hunting? This was an area that almost always gave me something when it came to bears, but at the time, I wasn't aware of this. Bear scat litters much of the road or any other spot you want to check out in late August all the way to the beginning of October.

I made my way to the spot from which I wanted to call and took off my pack. This was going to be a quick evening hunt, a favorite of mine for summertime bears. The heat of summer middays are best left for lakes and rivers, and evenings are for bear hunting! I put my back up against an old cedar stump, one of many littering the area. Partially rotted, it still supports life in the form of huckleberry bushes and even another cedar tree growing out of its top. I decided to let the area settle down a bit before I started to call, so I just sat and enjoyed the peace and quiet for a bit.

Much of the hunting area in my state of Washington is walk-in only. Clearly marked with signs, people know better. You are not allowed to use any motorized vehicles whatsoever past the gates. However, there are those who choose to ignore this law and, in turn, drive me and countless other hunters crazy. There is little more frustrating than hiking a few miles back and then having someone bust by you on a motorcycle or quad, illegally, and making a bunch of noise. So, as I sit there enjoying my time and getting ready to call, what happens? Two quads bust down the gravel road not more than 500 yards from my current position making all sorts of racket. My heart sunk . . . *sigh* . . . probably no chance of a bear showing up now. Oh well, I think to myself, I might as well call and give it a shot.

To either side of me is a tree line of mature trees, and the cut where the power line runs is about 100 yards across. These types of cuts are perfect for calling. With my heart slightly defeated, I started my predator calling with a favorite call at a low tone for about four or five minutes. I usually start calling a bit quiet so as to not blow out animals from the area. To my absolute surprise, here came a black blob out of the woods all the way to the bottom of the hill some 500 yards off. Keep in mind, this patch of woods is literally about forty yards from the same road those lousy quads came busting down. I was astonished that the bear would come out so shortly after the quads came by. I learned something that day.

As I put up my binos to view the bear, she crossed the lower grassy path and close behind was a yearling cub. Was I disappointed? Not at all. While I would not shoot a sow with a cub (who would do that knowingly anyway?!), I was very pleased to be able to watch them for the time being. She crossed below, right to left, and headed into the brush to work her way into the tree line. I kept calling, frantically at times. I wanted to see the bear again and see how close I could call her in. I kept watching the tree line to my left. There was plenty of space between me and the tree line, so I did not feel that the bear would be able to sneak up on me from this position without seeing it from about 100 yards off. Sure enough, she popped out with her little fellow close behind.

They appeared about 200 yards away, having worked up toward me in the safety of the cover of the trees. She worked her way through the brushy gulley to my left, which had a babbling brook snaking through it even this time of year. I kept calling, and she kept coming, not in a rush, just plodding along. At one point, the momma bear bounced over a fallen cedar tree from the uphill side of the log. There was a bit of a drop on the downhill side of the log. The cub faithfully followed momma but was hesitant about the log situation. It was about a five-foot drop and the cub paced nervously for a few seconds while getting up the guts to take the plunge. He got the guts and launched off that log like a kid headed into a lake from a dock. The little guy tumbled through the brush with the grace of me while trying to do the same thing . . . which, needless to say, isn't much grace at all. He rolled a bit and came upright. He made it through one of the day's trials without issue. To this day, I still smile thinking of that moment shared with the bears. I truly thank the Lord that I am a hunter and thanked Him for giving me the gift of that moment. It was funny to watch and a joy to remember.

As the cub caught up with momma bear, she ate brush and berries and just sauntered up closer and closer. As I called on the Sceery brand predator call, it seemed to me that she was more curious about the noise than a predator of the possible dying animal. She did not take any sort of stealth precautions and wasn't running in. I stopped calling as she got closer, and by then she just kept eating away—trying to build up that winter fat. A sow and cub are a dangerous combo. A sow is not something to be messing with, and even though she was not a huge bear, she still could have beat the living daylights out of me if she got close enough. With that in mind, I made sure she had plenty of escape routes to take. I did not want her or the cub to get too close to me and get startled, so at about thirty yards I stood up to let her know what I was by talking to her. She stood up in the brush and gave me a quick look in typical black-bear fashion, then made a run for the nearest heavy cover. She and the little bear made it to the safety of the thick, mature tree stands, while I was given the gift of the moment and the ability to walk back to the truck unharmed. It ended perfectly, and I was thankful for it. Plus, I had successfully called in a bear and filmed it, too, which was amazing to me!

Every encounter I have with bears teaches me something, and this situation was no different. First, I don't remember being able to watch a sow and cub before this instance, especially for that long. I soon realized it is one of my favorite pastimes. To watch a momma bear and a rambunctious little bear wander about is truly priceless as long as it is done at a safe distance. Second, I never would have guessed that I would call a bear out of the woods right after those quads busted through, but the sow proved me wrong. Hunting can be so unpredictable, you just have to love it.

PUP DISTRESS, AN UNCONVENTIONAL BEAR CALL

In the Calling Bears chapter of the book, you read about my theory on unconventional calling. This means don't always use the run-of-the-mill, standard rabbit distress or fawn distress call to get bears to come to you. Use a call someone else would not use, something new to the bear's ear, something unique, something interesting. This could be just the edge you need to bust that bear loose of the thick brush or dark timber it hides in. This story deals directly with that.

A couple weeks later, I went back to the same spot as the sow and cub I just wrote about. Like I said, it was and is a favorite bear location of mine. I headed back up to the very same stump from which I called the sow. On either side of me there was a tree line and a nice power-line cut with brush in the center. Some berries were still on the vine, and there was still plenty of scat about. So, I knew there were bears in the area.

When I call bears, I like to take the advice of the great Randy Anderson of Calling All Coyotes/Verminators fame, via Primos. Randy has advised to make up scenarios in your head when you call to make things more realistic.

An example would be to have a deer fawn getting hurt or stuck, so you use a fawn distress. Now after some time has passed, you add some coyote howls and barks to make it sound like coyotes have found the fawn. Then increase the intensity of the fawn distress to make it sound like it is getting torn apart by a pack of coyotes. Do you see where I am going with this? The call can be used in any variety of ways: a rabbit getting killed by a coyote, a coyote being killed by a wolf, and so on.

In this particular instance, I had a scenario of a rabbit getting killed by a coyote, therefore I was using what I had on hand—a closed-reed rabbit distress call along with my 'Lil Dog Primos coyote howler. I started the call sequence with a few coyote howls as best I could, then a minute later I started up with a rabbit squealing. So, any animal that hears this will think a couple of coyotes have got a rabbit and are getting a meal going. I was about twenty-five minutes into my set when I tossed in a few good coyote pup distress calls. If you are not familiar with how that might sound, imagine stepping on your dog's foot or tail by accident and you hear it yelp. Something along those lines, basically—a few quick, loud whimpers.

Directly after I did that, I glanced up and looked along the gravel trail to my right. What did I see but a large black bear barreling up the hill at me under thirty yards! It was a flash, but I distinctly remember the shoulders and butt of the bear bouncing toward me. Where did he come from? I thought with surprise. The trail the bear was on had an S curve with a stump directly in front of me. The stump was big enough to hide a bear—I'd say five feet tall and about that wide. When I first caught a glimpse of the bear, he was working his way up the S curve, but I lost him as he went behind the stump. I raised my rifle as he would be under fifteen yards by the time he came around the stump. I waited with my heart in my throat for what seemed like a very long five minutes or more.

I was running the scenario through my head as I sat there keen on every little noise or movement. He must have come from the wooded area on my right, downhill from the S curve stump area. I think then he stayed hidden in the brush until he decided to make his move when I hit the pup distress call. I sat there calling quietly trying to coax the ole boy out. Long moments passed; I was very tense. I called a bit more forcefully hoping to draw him out. My senses tingled, and I was hyperaware of my situation. It was like just narrowly avoiding a car wreck but still being stuck in the moment.

As time passed, I questioned whether or not I saw the bear or if it was just a figment of my imagination. More importantly, if it wasn't my imagination, where did it go!? After breathless moments, I decided to go investigate the bear's pathway. Sure enough, its tracks in the dirt gave credibility to what my eyes had told me. It was there and was running. Interestingly, when the bear got to the S curve and was able to get behind the stump, it used the stump as cover and slipped back into the brush, which lead to the timber. I never saw it on the other side of the stump in the brush, nor did I hear it. What an amazing creature. I loved it. Bears are incredibly cunning when they want to be and quiet as a mouse through some of the thickest terrain. They never cease to amaze me. Again, I wasn't able to shoot a bear this time around, but I did successfully call in a bear and had one heck of a story to tell.

As always, my hunting experience taught me a valuable lesson. Unconventional calling works well. Perhaps that bear had heard me call to the sow and cub with the rabbit call a few weeks before and had that particular call sound figured out. Then, when it heard the pup distress maybe it thought it was a different situation and decided to commit to coming in. Or perhaps it had snuck in and was waiting for the right time to come and bust up this family of coyotes in their feeding frenzy and take charge of the situation. I will never really know for sure. Furthermore, the simple fact that the bear was coming in full throttle, then paused after it got behind cover and either smelled me or saw something it didn't like, and was able to use the stump as cover to make its escape was impressive. You have to admit it, bears demand respect. What a worthy animal to chase! I am telling you these stories not only because I think they are noteworthy but I am also hoping to pass along some of my knowledge, mistakes, humor, and love of the animal off to you, so take it for what you will.

BLONDE BEAR SLOBBER!

Let me set the scene, here. It is the morning of August 1, 2009, the beginning to a hot day. We had an early start, and the crisp summer morning held promise. After all, it was opening day of bear season. My older brother, David, who loves to hunt bears as much as I do, was able to come along. He had his rifle, and I carried my hand-me-down Hoyt bow and, of course, a predator call around my neck. We drove out to a small community called Sultan, which is nestled at the base of glorious mountains leading up to Stevens Pass, a passageway that leads from western

Washington to eastern Washington. The surrounding beauty of Sultan is one to both admire and respect. Timeless craggy mountains tower over the town, which lay surrounded by lesser foothills that have been logged for the last hundred years or so—perfect bear country.

We arrived at yet another walk-in gated road. We gathered up our weapons, took a few quick drinks of water, and headed off for another bear adventure. I had hunted the area earlier that spring, when I was able to take a nice boar. It was a special draw tag that I filled, which helped us all out since I was able to scout a bit for the general bear season. I knew of a great spot, another power-line cut with a small creek running across it and trees on both sides. Close by was a great clear-cut area. Creek draws, you will find, are a favorite of myself and bears. Hunt them anytime you can. Remember, food, water, cover, and area.

We walked about a mile to the spot while taking our time and just enjoying each other's company as brothers do—at least when they get older and stop beating on each other. I told him I would call and he could keep watch with the hope of him getting a bear. I had already tagged out that spring, and although I had the option of a second bear, I wanting him to bag one. The day was bone dry even though it was still early morning. To boot, it had not rained in some time.

I set up in the tall grass, which was over my head as I knelt. This was not an ideal setup, but I was still a bit new to calling. The deer bed I was laying in did provide some concealment. David, however, was tucked slightly into the tree line, just on the edge while standing on a small boulder looking into the timber and watching down the cut. It gave him just a slightly elevated view of the area. He was maybe ten yards to my right. I didn't care for the situation, as it was far too easy for something to come bouncing in on me, but Dave was elevated and could see something coming. Now, if he could hit what was coming in . . . well . . . it's hard to say. (Just kidding, brother.)

Anyway, I started in again with my rabbit distress call. I called for about forty-five minutes, pausing now and again to try to allow enough time for Dave and me to hear for anything approaching. Nothing seemed interested, plus my knees had just about enough of sitting there. I decided to end the set. However, I did break one of my own rules—I didn't wait a while after I ended the set to stand up or move. Now, David was still looking down the cut and into the woods. I didn't know it, but David had spotted movement just before I decided to end my calling. As I could barely see Dave, and he had his back mostly to me, I didn't know he was onto something. Right as I ended the calling, I noticed Dave start to lose his balance off the rock, and he yelled out, "Shoot, dang it," in disgust. As he yelled this, I heard the brush bust up, and I knew something was very close.

"What was it?" I asked. "A bear, a blonde one!" Dave exclaimed. I had called one in and didn't even know it. Dave barely knew it. I asked him to fill me in. He said he didn't catch the movement of the bear until later in the set. He was able to watch the bear work its way closer to me, but the bear couldn't see what was making all the racket. So, through the trees, the bear worked its way to me by only moving while I called. If I stopped calling, the bear would stop. When I started to call again, the bear would start moving, very slowly, creeping like a cat on a stalk. This made it very difficult, if not impossible, to hear the bear when I stopped calling. This is an important point that will be mentioned throughout this book. Remember, the cadence of your calling can dictate how a bear comes in.

We had just missed the chance at a blonde bear! Oh, the agony! David felt the bear knew something was up but couldn't quite figure out what. Every time I would start calling, the bear would glance over at David's tall figure (more than six feet) and work his way toward me. According to him, the bear had gotten to within about five to seven yards of him and only about fifteen yards to me. Poor Dave, he had a bad angle on the bear. He was not able to turn and face the bear, nor was the bear going to step in front of Dave on the path it was taking. The bear was mainly behind and to the left of him. Dave watched as the predator put its stalk on me by creeping ever so slowly to within striking distance.

David decided to try to contort his body for a shot, but at that close range and silhouetted with the grass behind him, he had little hope. Plus, we Bozes have never been known for our balance, so he had that going against him. As he moved to try to get a better shot, the bear caught his movement, and Dave lost his balance, creating more movement. The rest, as they say, is history. The bear bolted.

After it was all said and done, I asked David to point out where the bear was coming in from. I could see why the bear was hanging out in the cool dark of the woods. The floor of the forest was absolutely covered in wild running vine blackberries, which were ripe. As I approached where the bear was making its stalk, I could see drips of water on some of the leaves of the blackberries—remember, it had not rained in some time, and there was no dew that morning whatsoever. It wasn't water at all, it was drool. The bear was drooling as it was coming to eat me! How cool is that!

This experience gave me some more knowledge about hunting bears. It confirmed that bears will often only come when called to and pause when the calling stops. This is not set in stone, but it is a fairly common stalking tactic that bears use. Second, I guess my brother is in no hurry to have me killed, since he had a pretty good opportunity to let the bear do so. Third, this gave me knowledge of a food source that ripened in the area before the other food sources became available, which is handy to keep in mind for future hunts. Moreover, I learned there are bears in the area now, too, not to mention a color-phase or blonde bear. Finally, it affirmed once again how quiet and darn sneaky bears can be when the want to be. They amaze me to no end. Do not assume bears are noisy or are easily spotted if they know something is up. They can disappear like a drop of water in a full bucket.

BEAR CALLED IN WITH A CALF CALL

Several years ago now, I was off hunting elk with my brothers, father, and a few friends in eastern Washington in the hills outside a town called Ellensburg. The hills that surround the otherwise fertile valley that Ellensburg is in are ancient lava flows that are rolling hills peppered with tall pine trees and broken up by the occasional creek and eroded rocky hillside that is steep enough to make you pant for breath. Archery elk season is notoriously warm for the first part, usually with hunting temps in the eighties or hotter. You probably have experienced it before—freezing in the morning, sweating by midday. It is a wonderful time to be out and about, and archery elk has become one of my favorite pastimes now.

In this instance, I had walked down a closed logging road that crept along a steep hillside. An old cow trail that meandered along the road was also marked with a ton of elk and deer tracks; it was a popular spot for the local ungulates. On the bottom of the gulley to my right was a creek. The opposite side of the gulley was very rocky and steep and looked like a great place for cougars. Pines and sage were all over, and the elk, at the time, were plentiful in this area. I had worked my way down to a watering hole, which was no more than a muddy seep that pooled long enough to make a pit for animals to catch a drink or roll in and that the wasps in the area used to gather enough mud to make a nest somewhere. All along the gulley bottom and edges, you could see rose hips that were bearing their telltale red fruit, a favorite of bears in this area. I heard an elk bugle deep and loud on the opposite hillside that I was on, and he sounded like he was only a couple hundred yards off, if that. So, I grabed the only call I had at the time, a calf call made by Sceery. I have called in bull elk with this before, so I decided to give it a shot. It had worked great before!

After sounding off on the call a few times, sounding lost and alone, I got the elk to bugle back, which got my blood pumping. The wind was perfect and in my face. As the elk bugled back, however, I heard some crashing down in the creek bottom, which I figured was another elk (this was my first mistake—assuming what the noise was). The bugling elk and I shared a few calls back and forth, but I just could not get the elk to commit to coming in. This did not deter whatever was making the noise in the creek bottom, however, and that sound of crashing brush kept getting closer and closer. I blew on the lost calf sound a few more times, and now the crashing was steady. Whatever it was, it was coming full on.

Quickly, I moved into position to set up for a shot. I settled in next to a stump with a small tree growing to the side of it, which helped conceal my outline and movement. It was not a horrible position, I thought to myself. I shot the range finder in the direction I thought the elk would come out—twenty-three yards. The sound of crashing brush and snapping twigs kept getting closer and closer, and my heart was in my throat pounding away in my chest. I swore whatever was coming would be able to hear my heart pounding. I quickly drew back my bow, as the elk would be on top of me in moments. As soon as I drew back, out popped a gorgeous black bear, much closer than I ranged, too. It was maybe a two-hundred-pound bear, about average for the area. I was too shocked to react, as I had it in my mind that it was going to be an elk. This was another mistake of mine that I would like to point out. I drew back on something that I was not sure about. I assumed it was an elk, but it was a bear. It could have just as easily have been a person. I was younger in my hunting career, and this taught me a valuable lesson that I have not forgotten. I should not have drawn back like that. Please make note of it.

As the bear crested the hill it was coming off of, it was only thirteen yards or so from my position. He paused briefly, a split second, and then continued to spring away into the clear-cut on the other side. I was stunned, and adrenaline was flowing. This was also the first bear I had seen with nothing more than my bow. At the time, it was not legal in the state of Washington to carry a sidearm when bow hunting even for protection. This regulation has since changed, thankfully. I took a breath and gathered

around looking for any sign of cubs. A minute or so passed and I walked up to the bear to confirm that it was a female. It was a smaller bear, one I probably would have passed on, but it all happened very quickly, and the end result was that I was walking away and it wasn't. I will take that any day. When I field dressed it, it was dry, and by that I mean it was not lactating. I spent some time looking for cubs but found none. My hope was it was either too young to have mated or just didn't have any cubs.

After field dressing, I opened up the stomach, which is something I do with bears to see what they have been eating in the area. This bear's stomach was solid and full of blackberries; it literally smelled like a berry pie. I was a mile or so back in, and it was getting dark. I hoisted the bear up onto my shoulders like an old lady would wear a fox scarf, kind of put it in a headlock, grabbed the rifle, and started the hike out. A murder of crows was beginning to form and head to their nightly roost as I watched the clouds change from pink to orange and then dark. In retrospect, I should have tied the two right paws together and the two left paws together, making it into a bear backpack, but I had not heard of this technique back then. I was able to struggle my way out, and I ended up at the truck after dark. My girlfriend at the time, who is now my wife, explained that I looked a bit rough with blood all over my shoulders from carrying it out, but I told her that was all part of the fun. She didn't see it that way.

All the animals I have killed hunting are special to me in one way or another. I don't care if it is a coyote, bear, or spike deer. They all mean something to me, and all are respected for what they are and what they gave. This bear was no different. I liked that white patch so much I got her half mounted, and she now sits proudly on my man cave wall. This was my first experience with a bear charge while not calling. This bear was a prime example of ground shrinkage, where a bear looks bigger than what it really is. After you shoot it and walk up on it, it shrinks or seems smaller than what you thought. Bears are notoriously hard to judge even for experienced hunters.

THE STUBBORN BEAR

This next story takes place on private property. It was a typical bear-hunting day in late August; the temperature was high, and there were plenty of berries hanging off vines. I hiked into a clear-cut that was about five years old.

It was perfect for bears—lots of cover, lots of food, a creek close by, everything about it said bear to me. I found an old logjam pile and was able to scurry my way up onto it without making too much racket. I was now overlooking a flat clear-cut area that backed up to a steep foothill. This foothill was too far off for shooting, but it was clear enough that I would be able to see if a bear came down through what was left of the standing trees.

The sweet smell of berries filled the air this time of year, as the whole woods smelled like cooking berries. It was wonderful. Not far off, I could hear the creek flow over the rocks. I allowed the area to settle down before I started to use the predator call. When I refer to letting an area settle down, I mean letting it return to its normal activity. Even if you are very quiet, you still alert the birds, squirrels, and other animals that you are there by the noise, scent, and movement you make. Sitting still for a bit before calling allows the natural sounds return to the area you are going to call into. The wind was calm, and the skies were clear blue. I had taken bears from this spot before, so I usually come prepared for some action. It is a favorite spring bear area of mine.

Dusk was approaching, and I decided to start calling. I started out low in tone, which is typical for me. I didn't want to just start blowing full force and freak things out, so I started like what a slightly wounded animal would do. Off in the distance, near the base of the steep foothill, was a line of Douglas fir trees that were about twenty-five feet or more tall. I could hear some noise coming from that area, which to me sounded like a bear tearing into a stump. I cannot be sure, but it definitely sounded that way. I decided to really start to let loose on my call with the hope of having the bear break cover. I let the call scream loud and raspy, which usually works pretty well.

Notice, I said *usually*. The bear sounded as if he were maybe seventy yards beyond the border of the trees that lined the clear-cut. I tried to break the bear loose for about thirty-five to forty minutes on the call by squalling away and making all sorts of noise. It was not having it. I could just hear the stump getting the brunt of its attention. The bear must have found a nice stump with some ants or grubs in it. I have noticed this behavior before with bears—if they are already on a food source, it can be hard to break them away from it.

The lack of commitment by the bear frustrated me. Why didn't the bear just come in and say hello, maybe stick its head out, or turn broadside at thirty yards? It's not asking a lot. But the bear had other ideas and stayed with the stump. Ever so slowly, I could hear the stump-tearing action quiet down, and it started to wander through the brush off to the left. I patiently waited a little in hopes that it would circle around and come investigate my noise, but of course it did not. By now, I had jokingly decided that if I did see this bear, I was going to shoot him out of spite, as it had frustrated me enough.

Dusk was settling in and coming fairly quickly. I decided it was time to go, as I still had some distance to cover before I could make it back to the truck, and even then, I had another hour drive home. So, I climbed down off my logjam as quietly as I could but not caring too much. After all, the bear wandered off. I worked my way to the path out and started to hike out. Nighthawks love this area for some reason. They make a "*zooooom*" sound when they skydive, particularly at dusk. They are great to listen to on the hike out. I didn't get more than 100 yards down the path when I saw a coyote that looked like it was coming in to see what all the predator calling was all about.

The coyote saw or heard me walking down the trail and was walking away from me at about sixty yards. Now, normally, I see a coyote, and I shoot the coyote. But this was summer, so the hide was no good, and my .300 WSM would not have left much of the coyote pelt anyway, so I passed on the shot. As I walked down the path, I got to about where I first saw the coyote. I was walking at a normal rate and not trying to be all that quiet. At that moment, I could hear some rummaging in the brush to my right. That bear was in the brush walking parallel to the trail I came in on. He was busting all sorts of brush, comfortable as all get out. Snorting and breathing loudly, he didn't have a care in the world.

Well, this was a turn of events, I thought to myself! Not far up the path, there was a T. If the bear continued on its current path, it would pop out on the trail right at that T, where I would be waiting for him. Oh, my heart rate started to pick up once again. Bear hunting, you have got to love it! Judging from the sounds the bear was making, it was very close. I could hear it snort and munch along, but the brush was so thick to my right that I could not see into it. Now, bears don't often listen to your plans of attack, and this bear decided to do its own thing, which seemed to be its trademark.

The bear, for whatever reason, decided to make a very sharp left turn, which would take him directly to me. Now when I first heard the bear, I was on the far right of the path. As it turned and started to get closer, I backed up three steps . . . one, two, three. The bear was snorting, and I could hear it chewing, breathing—it was going to be on top of me any second . . . and there it appeared literally three steps from my current position. If I had not moved, that bear would have stepped right on me. I had moved my rifle to my shoulder just before the bear popped out of the brush. All I could see was hair through the scope.

Adrenaline was coursing through me terribly. The bear, only steps away, looked at me and I at him; the moment seemed forever. I was motionless, trying to keep an eye on the bear through the scope while keeping my other eye on the bear who was steps from me. We both knew something was up; you could tell the bear had an uh-oh moment. *Boom*! I let the Mule kick. After I shot, it was an absolute tornado of pissed off black snarling mess that was tearing and biting. I froze. I was scared to reload and scared to move for fear of becoming the object of the bear's revenge. After a few spins with leaves and branches going everywhere, he bolted back into the brush. I could hear him growling as he moved back the way he came. I listened painstakingly for the telltale bear death moan but didn't hear it. I only heard the bear leaving my immediate area.

Darkness was falling and falling fast. I found a splattering of blood and hair on the blackberries where the bear had spun. I decided it would do me no good to go pushing the bear if I went after him now, especially in the dark or what would soon be the dark. I decided to walk out and track in the morning.

I drove home with thoughts of the bear on my mind, as well as what to do in the morning. I was regretting taking the shot. I was unsure of where I hit the bear, and shooter's remorse was poisoning my thoughts, but I tried to remain positive. I volunteered my little brother Johnny to help track. I say *little*, but I should say younger. Johnny is built like an ox, and he's taller than me at more than six feet with legs like trees and the ability to carry weight like a pack mule. He is handy in a pack out, for sure.

We arrived first thing in the morning. Johnny had a 12-gauge shotgun for close encounters, and I had my .30-.30 lever-action, open-iron-sight Winchester. I also carried some leather gloves and hand pruners, which are necessary equipment when diving into blackberry bushes after bears. We hiked into the area where I shot the bear and found the blood and hair. Johnny and I continued to search for blood or sign. The only sign we did find of the bear in that thick, nasty brush was a drop or two of blood just past where I initially shot the bear. While we were looking for the bear, I noticed that there was an amazing game trail that paralleled the main trail I came in on merely a few yards in the brush. This was the trail the bear was walking on before he cut over to where I was. We searched from morning till evening with no luck. That awful sinking feeling of losing an animal was becoming a reality. My only hope at this point was that I grazed the bear or hit it in a non-vital area. I want to emphasize that we did not take a look for an hour, find nothing, and give up. We slogged through brush and briars, frustration and scrapes—we gave it our best efforts. I continued to come back for the next several days to see if any birds would give away the bear's carcass, but I never did see any birds, which would indicate a dead animal.

To this day, I still regret that shot. I should not have fired, especially with a scoped rifle. I should have moved farther back, scared off the bear, or just kept firing once I did fire. Things happened extremely quickly, and I feel I made the wrong choice. Of course, I could have chosen differently and ended up with stiches all over my body, saying to myself, "I should have shot." I guess you just never know how things will end up. Hindsight is 20/20, of course. But, I can take solace in this fact—I lost the bear, I gave it my all, and I hope that in sharing this story, others will learn from my mistake. Also, I hope that others will follow my example and give their fullest effort when looking for a wounded bear. The animal deserves it even though it can be dangerous, frustrating, nerve-racking, and crazy at times. Not every hunt is successful, not every stalk works out, and it is not like television hunting shows—this is real. Mistakes are made, and the only thing we can do is learn from them and not repeat them.

I also know how incredibly tough animals are. They can sustain damage from attack and somehow continue to function. This is another reason why I am so amazed at animals I have hunted or just generally see in the wild. I would bet dollars to doughnuts that the bear recovered from the shot. A taxidermist I know once told me that any really big bear he gets into the shop usually has one bullet-wound scar in its hide from a previous experience. I am not sure how accurate that is, but it leads me to believe that bears are tough animals.

INSTANT BEAR, JUST ADD CALLING

This bear-hunting spot is one of my favorites. It has its flaws, but during the month of September, it is usually a gimme spot for bear. The area is lined with power-line cuts, which means usually mature stands of trees (cover), brush under the power lines (food), and since it is western Washington, water is not too far off. Power-line cuts equal bear gold mines, in my opinion, and are my main go-to spots if I can find good ones.

I had hunted this location a few times already that year, but I was never able to seal the deal on a decent-sized black bear I had seen working the area. Once I spotted the bear working the edge of the trees and eating away contently at the berries along the tree line edge. Then, on another occasion, I spotted what I believed to be the same bear crossing the gravel road from one mature tree line to another in the direction of a small swamp. Bears were in the area, so I kept on coming back.

After I arrived at the walk-in gate, I hiked in about a mile or so. The area in which I had seen the bear had a small hill where you could look down into the power-line area before entering. As I arrived at the hillside, I paused, listened, and glassed for a bit with the binoculars. There were occasional stumps in the brush under the power lines, but from what I could tell, nothing was moving. It was a calm evening and the wind was light, if blowing at all. Just another lovely late summer bear hunt filled with the smell of berries and the chance of success. The only thing promised was a good time.

As I did not see any bears in the area, I decided to creep my way down past the swamp near the bottom of the hill and climb up on a stump. I had my typical day pack with me, some leather gloves on, and my .30-.30 Winchester rifle. I like to bring it along bear hunting sometimes; I like to call it going cowboy. It is just nostalgic to *not* have a scoped rifle on your arm.

So, I worked my way to the older cedar stump I wanted to call from. I was able to slink my way through the brush with not too much sound disturbance. I scurried up the stump so I was off the ground about four or five feet. I had a nice view of the tree line, which was about seventy yards in front of me with brush to each side of me for several hundred yards. I brought along with me a nice predator call that I had custom-made with elk antler. The closed-reed call made a nice raspy sound. Great for bear. I sat for a few minutes before I started. One thing I should point out: I brought along a mix of old and new ammo. The older ammo I had sitting around the house for some time—years, actually. I figured it would be okay, as it was stored in a dry place, but it did show signs of being old. I was proved wrong.

I started out with a medium volume on my antler call. The sound easily penetrated the trees close by and permeated the area surrounding me. The wind was still, so the sound carried nicely. Almost immediately, I caught movement to my right. To my immediate right was a nice-sized cedar stump surrounded with waist-high blackberry bushes and huckleberries, not to mention your basic field grass. I remember thinking, "That stump just moved," for a split second. Of course, stumps generally do not move on their own. The object that did move was very close to the same color of the stump—kind of an off-red color. I lifted up my binoculars and checked the movement, which was maybe fifty yards away. Sure enough, out came an absolutely gorgeous color-phase black bear with a reddish-blonde coat. I quickly brought out my little pocket camera, as I wanted to get footage of the bear.

As the bear slowly walked closer, I puffed lightly on the call to keep it interested. As soon as I called a bit more, the bear stood up at about forty yards on its hind legs. I was able to get that moment on film and couldn't believe that the bear was so close as I was hiking in. The bear dropped to all fours after giving me a stare down and continued on into the call. I set the camera down and got into position for a shot.

As I raised up the rifle, the bear stood on its hind legs again. I centered the open iron sights on the bear and squeezed the trigger. The crack of the gun sent the bear to the ground. He was swirling on all fours, biting, and snarling. I quickly worked the lever action and shucked another round into the chamber. I took aim at the bear but hesitated to fire. The bear quit spinning and began to work his way to the tree line, which was absolutely chocked with brush. I did not want the bear getting into that mess. I knew it was a tangled mess of thorns, devil's club, and felled logs, as I helped my brother recover a bear from the same patch of woods a few years back.

I steadied on the bear's left shoulder and—*pow*—fired again. Although the rifle didn't go *pow*, it went *click* instead. Misfire! Old ammo! So much for relying on that old stuff. I was stunned but quickly recovered and slammed another round into the rifle. This time, however, the cartridge jammed. Looking back, I don't think I worked the lever action all the way open; it was just enough to start to get the other round in, which caused the jam. No matter what, I had a jammed rifle with a wounded bear at about thirty-five yards on the move away from me. I had to quickly remedy this situation.

After some quick fumbling, I was able to clear the jam and get another cartridge in. Aiming once again for the left shoulder, I fired and this time heard the report of the round going off. The bear shuddered at the impact. But the bear kept moving. I slammed another round in, fired at the shoulder, and watched the impact. The bear crumpled on the ground, and I thought, Finally, the bear is down!

To my astonishment, the bear slowly began to crawl away with its left shoulder undoubtedly broken. The bear had taken a direct hit into the chest and two rounds into the left shoulder, how was it still moving? It was an absolute testament to the might of bears. I had one more round left in the rifle. As it was working its way to the tree line, I put another round into the chamber and took careful aim to make this the end shot. I squeezed the trigger and . . . click. *Arrggg!* There was not another round in the rifle; I must have ejected two rounds when I was clearing the jam. I watched as the bear belly crawled and reached the safety of the tree line cover. I was none too pleased with this turn of events.

Stunned, I ran through the events of the last few minutes. I really couldn't believe it. I went from not thinking a bear was close by to having one within a stone's throw to firing at a bear, getting my rifle jammed, and running out of ammo only to watch such a gorgeous bear crawl into a ton of hiding places in the deep, dark woods. Disgusted is the word that came to mind. Undeterred, however, I hopped down off my perch after waiting several minutes for the bear to expire.

Judging from the sound of the bear, it just made it into the tree line. I didn't hear any further noise once it got to the trees. Perhaps it just went into the brush and died. Or perhaps it was balled up under a log while waiting for me to come in there so it could pounce on my butt? Could go either way. I found the blood trail with ease. It was good blood, lots of it, and the bear was literally dragging itself into the brush, so the trail wasn't too tough to follow. I checked my cell phone, and I had several missed calls (I always put my phone on silent when I go hunting). A family emergency came up, and I had to leave almost immediately. Darkness was not too far off, so before I left, I marked the trail with some toilet paper. I scurried into the dark woods with my pistol drawn on high alert. I didn't notice much of a trail once I got into the woods, which seemed very odd to me. Out in the open of the power-line clearing, it was nearly dusk; in the woods, it was nearly dark. The hair on my neck was standing straight up, and I had an uneasy feeling about this. I searched for about twenty minutes with the hope of quickly finding it. It was now dark in the woods, and I needed to go to tend family, but I needed to find this bear, too. I am not the kind of hunter who would shoot something and leave it; I believe most hunters aren't. I was sick about the bear and sick about the family situation.

I ended up marking the trail and calling my brother, who said he would come out first thing in the morning with his friends and search the area for the bear. I was relieved with that, knowing that I had to leave for the other side of the state as soon as I got back to the house. The fact that my brother was willing to go into brush looking for a wounded bear gave me comfort. It is not something I would normally ask of a person, since it can be very dangerous. I have done it for him, so I guess it was his turn.

The next morning found me in Idaho dealing with the death in the family. I called my search party throughout the day for updates. My brother and four of his friends all found blood and the toilet paper I left as a marker but were unable to find the bear. Four people searched for more than eight hours, often on hands and knees, and were unable to locate the bear. I was sickened by it. I desperately wanted to be back there looking; I hated that I could not be. Of course, I would not have missed what I had to attend, either. It was just a crap sandwich, and I had to take a bite of it.

I was able to return to the site three days later after I buried our loved one. The last two days, it had rained very heavily and washed away any trace of blood. I went back to my trail and saw all the work the boys had done. The brush was stomped down everywhere, marker tape covered the area in a grid pattern—it was obvious much effort was made, and for that I was very grateful. I searched that evening with no luck. I then returned the following week looking for any sign of the bear or birds that might give away its rotting carcass. Again, nothing. I decided to notch my bear tag and call it quits that season. I believe that bear died, but I could not be sure. In my thought process, that was my bear, and my tag was filled. I was not going to go back out to try to fill my tag. It was filled.

About not finding an animal, I do know this—nature allows nothing to go to waste. That bear, if it did die, fed birds, coyotes, another bear, and countless other bugs that then fed other animals. Losing an animal is a bitter, tough pill to swallow. If you hunt long enough, though, it will happen to you. That is why it is called hunting and not grocery shopping. Things happen: ammo doesn't shoot, you miss vitals, your arrow hits an unseen twig, and so on. Notching my tag was my own way of dealing with the situation—that and demanding better of myself.

Again, hunting taught me a valuable lesson. Don't use old ammo, for one. Dispose of it at the range. Also, I should have waited for a nice broadside shot instead of taking a chest shot. While it is not a horrible shot, it was not the best shot to take. The other shots I took at the left shoulder were pretty good shots, but the bear was quartering away just slightly. Shot placement is key for any animal but bears especially. They just seem to be tougher than the rest. If a bear is moving, keep firing until that bear is not moving. Trust me, I have been after enough bears in the brush to realize it is not something you want to do on a regular basis.

This experience also hammered home the joys of predator calling. I would have had no idea that bear was so close had I not used a predator call. Maybe the bear was bedded down in the area, or maybe it was just eating away at a bush, I will never know. But what I do know is that the bear showed up because I used a predator call. Calling for bears works!

BEARS IN THE SNOW!

This next story is a favorite of mine involving my older brother, David; clear, cold gorgeous weather; and snow-covered rugged peaks. I think there was a bear or two involved, too, but that is secondary, of course. Well, not really! Hunting in the North Cascades of Washington is amazing. The mountain peaks are rugged and terrible, the terrain can be steep and unforgiving, and the views are breathtaking. Even without any success, going bear hunting in the fall in these mountains is a wonderful reward.

My brother and I decided to make a last-ditch effort on the second-to-last weekend of bear hunting one season. Bears can be hard to find later in the season—many bear hunters just plain give up after mid-October, but boy are they missing out (our season in Washington goes until November 15). When it is cold, snowy, and getting icy, it can be a wonderful time to call bears. Hides are prime, bears are hungry, and you never know what might happen when your back is turned.

We got up early and drove the hour-plus to where we wanted to park before we started to hike in. The area is not too far from a hill my other brothers affectionately call Operation Certain Death, a steep, nasty hill laden with mountain blueberries, cliffs, and avalanche chutes. We have all sorts of different code names for the areas we hunt—One Buck Hill, Hill from Hell, Doug's Canyon, Big Buck Canyon, the Brushy, and so on. The drive there was filled with hot coffee, old-fashioned doughnuts (we are hunting, after all), and small chitchat about who is the better hunter and so on, as brothers do. It was great.

We arrived at the parking area, and the sun was just starting to showcase light in the sky. We were surrounded by jagged peaks on either side of us. Snow covered the ground at a depth of about two feet or so. Our truck was plowing through the untouched snow. Ice crystals sparkled in the air and shined like glass as they floated about carelessly on the bone-chilling breeze, which was ever so slight. I had never hunted this area before, so it was all new to me. It looked pretty amazing, so I was anxious to get to calling.

David led the way, and we marched a mile or so down the trail. Now, the trail was more like an ice luge; obviously popular with hikers, the trail had been packed down, but the surrounding area was all but untouched fluffy snow.

My brother had not gotten out to hunt much that year, so I was more than willing to go call for him. I brought my rifle with me but really just wanted him to be successful. Of course, I would not have paused if I saw a bear, but it wasn't a priority. He really just needed a predator caller, so by now you know what I wanted to do! Call away!

Our hike started out along a rocky creek bottom; to either side of us the foreboding mountain sides rose up and caged us in. The creek below trickled softly down the canyon, which was the only sound on the otherwise quiet morning. Do you know the quiet I am speaking of? Have you walked outside after a fresh snow in the mountains? It seems so quiet that your ears are just straining to hear something. It was like that except the cold was biting my ears, so I had the tips of them buried under my stocking cap.

We plugged along the trail for about another mile and enjoyed the postcard scenery. As we walked along, the trail went in and out of tree clusters only to reveal a steep, rocky, treed area to our left and a wide expanse of valley floor where the creek ran on our right. On either side of the creek was various brush, vine maple, devil's club, and the remnants of blueberries. Above the creek on the far side of us was the sloped valley wall. We decided to stay on our side of the valley floor, since going across the tangle below left a lot to be desired. In addition, there were obvious open fissures and dangerous cracks in some of the year-round snow that was on the other side. We would be just as well staying on this side.

On the far side of the valley across the creek, there were clumps of pine trees. Not a lot of them, mind you—maybe a clump of ten or twenty trees that happened to take hold and survive between avalanches. Along the creek bottom, you could see where there were sets of what I believed to be bear tracks that would lead from the bottom by the creek up to these clumps of trees. It looked as if the bears were traveling from the creek bottom to the clumps of trees but did not leave. Essentially, each one of those clumps of trees looked as if it might have a denning bear in there, so I affectionately called them bear apartments. It was really curious to see how one trail would lead up to the trees and there would be no exit trail. You would look at the next clump, and the same thing. Amazing.

You can see what I like to call bear apartments on the right-hand side of the picture. Those clumps of trees hide bears denning up, or at least that is what I expected. No bears came out of those dens from my calling, but some certainly came from behind!

With those tracks and that terrain, my strategy basically wrote itself. We were going to plant ourselves on this side of the valley, call over to the suspected den areas, and have the bears come to us. A simple plan, which seemed pretty solid to me. I had no desire to have to cross that icy creek, so I would have the bears do it. The sound of the call would easily reach the several hundred yards it was from us to the bear apartments, especially on this cold, crisp, calm morning.

Now, behind us we had a rocky slope with a creek that fed the lower creek, scattered brush, and, at the top of my viewing, mature trees. I did notice a few mountain goats on the cliffs above us, as well. I love those animals! I decided to tuck myself into some frozen devil's club just off the icy path we walked in on. I was on kind of a blind curve of the trail, which offered a good view of the valley but not so much of the back trail. It was not the coziest of areas, but it would work. It was not ideal for me, as I normally like a solid background to rest against for protection. But my thought was if something came for me, it would have to make some noise to get through all this brush, so I would have time to react. I had a nice view to my left and some view to my right of a couple of the bear apartments.

My brother followed down the creek that fed into the lower creek. He was just below me and to my right, slightly out of sight, say 100 yards away. He was almost to the creek bottom, actually. Although I could not see him, he was aware of my positioning, and I was aware of his. Safety first. I had a good view of the valley, of the two bear apartments, and of some decent firing lanes. One thing was for sure, you couldn't beat the scenery.

I decided to get started calling once I was sure Dave was in position. It was very chilly that morning. I started out typically quiet on the call, again, hoping not to blow animals out of the area. I figured at the least we would get a coyote to come in. Eventually, I worked up my calling tempo and frequency for about twenty minutes, really letting loose on it. Nothing popped out of those bear apartments. Man, I had a feeling those things would have produced something, but if there were a bear in there, perhaps it realized it was just too nice and cozy to get out of the den on that morning—and for that I could not blame it.

The cold was steadily draining the feeling from my hands, my lips didn't want to curl around the call, and I was getting pretty chilly. I had only been calling about twenty minutes when I decided to stand up and check behind me to see if anything was coming down the trail. I had to stretch just a little bit and try to work up some heat. Normally, I wouldn't cut the calling session so short, but it was bone-chilling cold out.

Since I was not seeing anything move, I stopped calling and stood up. I checked the area behind me and looked up the canyon, though I was not seeing anything worthwhile. I was expecting more than this, I thought to myself. I held in place and wiggled my toes and flexed my legs trying to get some blood moving to warm my lower body. I did this for a minute or two. Not seeing anything coming in, I sat back down on my pack and started calling at a frantic pace again. I had to try to keep my reed from freezing in my call as the moisture from my breath was causing it to lock up at times. This is not uncommon in very cold weather.

I called heavily for about another ten minutes. My knees again reminding me of the joys of standing up. I was getting colder and more anxious as time passed, and I was at least expecting to see a hungry coyote come bolting out from somewhere—come on! I decided I had had enough and stood back up. As soon as I did, I heard a muffled shot bounce off the canyon walls (the sound of a shot, not a bullet itself)! My brother had shot his .338. Surprised, I bounced up out of the devil's club and got to the icy trail. I worked the few feet down the trail to the corner and asked, "What did you shoot?!" I was thinking it would be a coyote only because we really were not calling for too long, and usually coyotes don't take too long to come in.

David responded, "Black bear, stay there. I don't know if it's down yet." I stayed put but positioned myself so I could see David just downhill about forty yards from my position, and he was pointing uphill. I looked uphill behind me and didn't see anything. Granted, he was not pointing in my immediate direction. After a few seconds, he gave the all clear, and then he explained what I could not have possibly known without him there.

When I first stopped calling, David had the same idea I had—we were both freezing and decided to stand up. So, Dave stood up, and on the trail just above him was a black bear walking directly toward my position just around the corner from me. The bear was a larger bear who was sniffing the air as it was coming at me—literally about fifteen feet behind my blind spot. I never saw or heard this bear. As David stood up, the bear, who was coming to eat me, caught Dave's movements and lumbered back around and down the trail away from me. David, being ice cold and having a bit of bear fever, was unable to get a bead on the bear as it wandered away. I could see David's reaction now in my head; I wish I could have seen it in person. I am sure some choice, salty words were thought or mumbled under his breath at the time.

So, being excited but frustrated, David decided to walk up the hill to the trail with the hope of being able to see the bear and get a shot. When Dave was marching up the snow-covered creek bed, I began to call again (completely unaware I just had a bear at fifteen feet behind me). As David continued his defeated march up the hill, after a few minutes, he happened to glance up the hill to see another black bear, smaller than the first, coming into my ongoing calls. This bear was about forty yards up the hill from me on a small ledge by the creek that trickled down the hillside. The bear was quite intent on all the noise I was making and failed to see David. The bear would stop when I would stop calling and then start coming in when I would start calling again. This is a very key point, which I hope you have picked up by now.

Calling constantly or as much as possible is key when you're calling bears. Time and time again, I have seen them stop when I stop and go when I call. Keep that in mind when you are giving this a try. Take only short breaks to catch your breath or listen for incoming bears. Call as often as you can.

My brother David had the pleasure of watching the bear get up on its hind legs while sniffing and trying to figure out where I was. Since I was tucked into the brush below the bear, the slope of the hillside likely blocked the bear's view of me. Again, I was completely unaware of any of this happening. The bear plopped down on all fours and continued its search for a nice winter meal—me. The bear happened to turn broadside, and David let loose with his rifle to end the bear's life in one shot. The bear was hit solidly but still had enough in it to charge about fifteen yards or so downhill before piling into a heap in the rocky creekbed. I think the bear running was just a flight response; I don't believe it to be an aggressive response.

The bear my brother shot, which was in the snow when we found it—a fantastic view of a bear down with some amazing peaks in the background.

Once he told me the story, I was surprised to say the least. I couldn't believe I had a bear at such a short distance behind me without seeing or hearing it. If I were calling alone, I would have likely never seen the bear and thought I never called anything—provided it didn't pounce on me. That bear died on a crystal-clear, freezing-cold day. It was my first I had called in while, there was snow on the ground, and I was able to call a double, no less! It remains one of my very special hunting memories that I made with my brother. Those of you who have been able to share hunting with your friends or family know exactly what I mean. Hunting with family and friends is truly a blessing.

We hiked up to the bear, and what a glorious coat it had. Very thick and full, jet black, and I would say four inches long or so. I checked the stomach contents, as I always do with bear, and it only had a fist-sized pile of plant material in it. It was hungry, that's for sure. So, hunting is all fun and games until you shoot something. Now the work begins. We gutted the bear on the spot but had about two miles to go in the snow to get the bear out.

On the way out, we enjoyed the scenery once again, were greeted by mountain goats, and ran into some hikers who were there to enjoy that same scenery. Some of them were amazed there were bears in the area, which I find quite humorous. I am not sure where they think bears live, but I can assure them, there are plenty in that area. One couple was so taken aback that bears were around that they left the trail and went back to the car. They must not have seen the posted signs at the trail head warning of bears.

On another note, some of the hikers were very curious and were amazed to see the bear. We spent a bit of time talking to those interested. I always like to take the time to discuss hunting with those who may be riding the fence on the idea of it. I think we left them with a pretty positive experience. The icy trail turned out to be quite the blessing on the way out. The bear slid easily down the trail once we got it there, and it only lost a few hairs on the way out. Another great memory for the record books!

My brother with his fine bear.

BY CHANCE, A BEAR!

This was another late-summer hunt in 2013. I was hunting another favorite spot of mine, which was actually not far from where my brother Dave and I called in a blonde bear. This area was a nice gas-line cut with mature trees on either side and a creek that gently rolls down the ravine. Have you noticed a pattern here? I like to find creeks with open areas and mature trees to call into. It is only a mile or so from where I have to leave my vehicle, which is nice. If you are hunting on hot days, leave yourself enough time to be able to get the bear out of the woods before the hide goes bad, for example, if the hair starts to slip. In addition, you need to consider how you are going to get the meat out and keep it cool. Know your limits.

So here's what happened. I veered off to the right at a junction and started the walk up the gravel road. There was a slight hill that I had to crest before I could look down into the creek bottom, which ended up being about 100 yards away or so. As I crested the hill, unexpectedly, I spotted a nice large bear walking from right to left about 125 yards out. He was moving from one set of mature trees to the next and eating some grass as he lumbered along. If I would have pulled up and fired, I would have had time to get a shot. But this time around, I wanted to try to get the shot on camera; with that in mind, I took off my backpack, got out my pocket camera, and set it up. By the time I got ready, the bear was disappearing into the woods to its left.

Still set up, I decided to try to entice the bear to come my way. I grabbed my predator call, which was around my neck (how I usually carry it just in case), and let out a few rabbit squeals. So my current situation was that I was lying on the ground, my gun on my pack, facing the direction in which I saw the bear, calling away. My hope was that the bear would hear the noise, get curious, and pop back out where it entered the woods. But the bear was smart and decided to use the woods as cover, which allowed it to close the distance and see, from the safety of the trees, what all the noise was.

I called for about ten minutes, and didn't really hear much of anything, and I started to lose a bit of hope. Then, off to my left about forty yards away, if that, I heard some noise. The noise was best described as if you were standing on a fallen rotted log, but the log was not strong enough to hold your weight, so it slowly crumbled and broke in half. I was picturing in my head that the bear was standing on a log, and it did just that—crumbled under its weight as it stood listening.

So, I pointed my rifle straight ahead down the grass cut, but it needed to be more off to my left. I could hear the bear close the distance slightly, getting closer. The tree line was maybe twenty yards to my left or right, and the bear sounded like it was within twenty-five yards of my position. I had to move, and move slowly, in case the bear came out of the woods. I shuffled and repositioned as best I could and hoped not to draw attention. I used the call in my mouth to help muffle the unnatural sounds of my scurrying in the grass. I then waited and listened.

I could hear the bear rustle a bit in the woods; his low growls made the hair on my neck stand up. There is something about being in close proximity to a bear on ground level that can really heighten your senses. I called some more, frantically, and hoped the bear would bust out of the brush to no avail. I called for about fifteen minutes, and slowly, throughout that time, I heard less and less of him. The jig was up, he had left the area. Oh, what a way to start the evening hunt!

This was yet another example of a bear hanging up in cover and the hunter being unable to get him to come out. Judging from the size of the bear when I first saw it, I would say it was definitely a mature boar, and it was likely not his first rodeo. The area I was hunting gets hit pretty hard by the local hunting population, so it may have been educated before. Plus, it may have caught my movement when I had to reposition, which I think a blind man could have seen, especially with the lack of cover I had and the proximity of the bear. Once again, I was bested by a bear, which is nothing to be ashamed of. They are magnificent animals.

The other point here is to take the time to hit your old hunting grounds. Yes, that place does have hunters and hikers coming through it quite often, but who knows how often it gets called into or if the bears have even been called to. Like in deer hunting or elk hunting if you have seen your quarry in an area before there is a reason they are there. Food, water, other like species, and so on. Don't be afraid to check out old haunts throughout the season, as you never know what you may find there. I ended up not tagging a bear that season, but it wasn't for lack of effort or chances; it was just hunting, and that means you might not always place a tag on an animal—which is how it should be.

ANOTHER HANG UP!

Shall I set up the scene again? Want to guess it? Yes, there is a creek nearby, yes there are clear-cuts, and, yes, it is early September. That is such a great time to be out in the woods. I had worked some logging roads, saw some occasional sign, but was more than content with walking slowly, listening to the birds sing me their song, and eating blackberries along the way. I was not seeing a lot in the way of bear sign, but that was okay. A doe and I stared at each other for some time as she worked the tree line's edge about 150 yards off. Simple pleasures of just taking in the scenery of the outdoors sure beat watching television.

Dusk was about an hour away. The wind had brought along some clouds that were a bit dark, a reminder that the dryness of our summer was getting ready to give way to the long rain of the Northwest fall and winter. By this time of the year, I welcome the rain and wind—after all, that means deer season!

I cut up an old logging-road spur and noticed right away that the road was littered with various bear scat, which varied from very fresh to a few weeks. A bear was working the area for sure, and you could see why. Either side of the road had brush that was up to ten feet high in spots with various berry bushes scattered all over, and there was a creek about a five-minute walk from my position. With a bit more purpose now, I wanted to work my way about 250 yards up the road to a logjam that overlooked a clear-cut and had the overgrown brush edge, a mature tree stand, and, less visible, a swamp area to the rear. Since I was finding sign, this put a bit of a jump in my step. I climbed up the logjam and tucked myself into the pile. Try to keep yourself from being silhouetted; if you can break up the outline of your body, do it.

I was facing the clear-cut and overgrown brush edge, which gave me the best views of the area. I was also able to see the closed-out gravel-road section that cut though the area, which would allow me to spot any coyotes or careless bears that would venture out. It is not uncommon for coyotes to take the path that requires the least amount of effort to get to the caller.

I began my calling session as I typically do, by starting off a bit on a low tone while working up to more of a frenzy. I used the mouth call for about twenty-five minutes when I heard a squirrel start to give off its warning chirp. Nature will tell you a story, you just have to listen to it. That squirrel was letting me know something was coming, whether it was a deer, bear, or another hunter. If a squirrel starts to sound off, especially a few hundred yards or less from your position, focus your attention on that area. Something is coming in. You have probably already read this hint, but it is one that cannot be overstated.

With the squirrel giving me the alert, I shifted my weight and body to focus more to my left, which was where the alert was coming from. I lifted up my knee to rest my gun on it to allow a more secure shooting position. I was now focused on the squirrel and continued to call, stopping only to listen for more brush sounds or more alerts from other squirrels. You can often hear the animal on its path coming to the call. A squirrel several hundred yards out may give the alert. Sometime later, another squirrel might belt out the warning a hundred yards closer or so, and so on. As the bear or coyote or bobcat gets closer, so do the squirrel alerts.

After a few minutes, I usually (and finally) get further confirmation that something is coming in. I hear a good-sized twig snap. Oh man, my heart always gets pumping when I know something is coming to a call. About seventy yards out, I heard the brush rustle for sure, twigs snapped— something was working its way to me—and the closer the sounds got, the faster my heart was beating. Anticipation is half the fun.

I quieted my calling just a little bit but still gave an urgency to it. I could hear whatever it was getting closer and closer—sixty yards, fifty yards, more breaking, closer squirrel alerts, forty-five, and then forty yards. My heart was in my throat. I always wonder what it could be until I see it. It was now just inside the clear-cut overgrown brush area—just out of full sight but easily within shooting range. Low growls could be heard as it paced back and forth, irritated that it would have to leave the brush to eat whatever was screaming and dying.

More branches broke, the growls increased, and it sounded pissed off that it had to break cover. I could hear it slapping trees and growling at me, but I couldn't see it. It had hung up in the brush, and the bear's better sense caused it to stay hidden. Dang clever bears, they drive me nuts! It had taken a bit of time for the bear to work its way to me, and dusk was beginning to lay over the once-vibrant day. Although the bear was within bow range, I had not shot. I could see branches move and still hear the bear, but he just would not commit. I called a little bit more and decided to stop with the hope that the bear would come out to see if the screaming animal had died.

I waited. I could still hear the bear but no luck. He wasn't buying it. Even though it was still legal shooting light, it was almost too dark to shoot. I decided to call it a night. I was a bit nervous climbing down off the stump pile with such an agitated bear within range, but I scurried down anyway. As I walked out, I checked my back trail a few times to make sure I was not being hunted by what I believe was a bear that I left pissed off and hungry. A swarm of mosquitoes forced me to quicken my pace back to the truck. I reran the scenario through my head: what could I have done differently? If another person was with me, perhaps, I could have set the other person more downwind of me, and they would have been able to get off a shot. Regardless, I was able to get back to the truck only suffering a few mosquito bites. Just another fine evening in the woods. I would really like to find the secret to get a bear to break cover consistently. I have read that an increased calling sequence does it; but, again, it is only on occasion. Heck, stopping a call can sometimes get bears to come out on occasion. The point is to get them to come out of the brush consistently; when I figure that out, I will be sure to let you know my secret. So stay tuned to me working that out, and I will let you know the results.

Another quick point about this story I'd like to include: I feel I was about two weeks late getting to this spot to hunt. Even though I believe a bear was there (the one I called in), I could have been hitting the spot earlier in the month. I say this because of all the sign that was in the area. That said, I will be sure to hit that area a bit sooner in the year or at least keep it in mind as one I want to seek out. Keep a journal of good spots you find or a mental note of bear sign and the time of year you found it and so on.

THE BACKSIDE OF THE HILL

Late August of 2012 found me just outside a town called Mount Vernon, which is not far from my home and hometown of Stanwood, Washington. This little-known spot is one of my little brother Jim's go-to areas for a quick evening hunt. We decided to meet up at about 4:30 p.m. to see what trouble we could find out there. Now, this spot is hunted a bit, hiked, and used for horseback riding plenty, but we were aware of those issues.

We walked into the area together. Jim had his bow, and I brought along my .30-.30 Winchester (yes, with new ammo). I used to change Jim's diapers, and now we hunt bears together; you have to really appreciate the blessings of family. He decided to take the fork to the right, which led up to a nice bowl followed by a large hillside and various clear cuts. I took the fork to the left, which had some mature trees and various fingers you could walk onto to look down into a few ravines that had been clear-cut. Either way, we were likely to see something.

As I walked along slowly and tried to remain quiet, I took notice of the bear scat littering the road, the berry bushes looking like somebody had thrashed them with a stick (but upon close inspection, the bear hair I saw on the thorns gave that story away), and just generally enjoyed the afternoon. As I climbed to the peak of the hill, I came across two women horseback riding. I said hello and stepped aside to allow a wide berth for the horses to pass. I mentioned I was bear hunting, and they seemed surprised. They continued past me, and I decided I would head back down to take a peek along some of those finger trails.

As I worked my way down the hill, I cut off onto a logging-road spur that ended up on a landing, which is a flat piece of land where loggers set up equipment to drag trees up the hill. (At least that is the way I understand it. I could be wrong; I am no logger.) So, there I was enjoying the backside view of the Skagit Valley. I worked my way softly down the ravine a few yards and stopped on top of a stump to get an elevated view of the area with mighty Mount Baker in the background. Then, I took notice of what was directly below me. The very stump that I just hopped on had been freshly torn into by a bear. The ants scurrying around in a disorganized frenzy confirmed this. A bear was probably pretty close by, I thought to myself.

No sooner had this thought occurred to me than did I notice, about twenty yards below me, that a bear was eating at a huckleberry bush. I should point out that I assumed it was a bear because at this point, I did not see the bear but the circumstances certainly pointed to a bear in the brush as it moved. An important note for any hunters reading this: When you see brush move, never shoot at it! I would never do that, and we hunters *must*, above all, be 100 percent sure of our targets. Do not brush shoot at anything. Now, let us continue. . . .

I observed these bushes moving for less than a minute when I caught flashes of black fur glistening in the sunlight. I saw a paw come up and grab some berries, I saw the bear move side to side—it was pretty great just to sit and watch. I wanted to try to get the bear up out of the brush so I could get a shot. I guess I could have waited for it to move out away from the brush, but I didn't have the patience, I guess.

It was about 7:30 p.m. by now, and in the background I could faintly hear the *clippty-clop* of the horses as they carried the two ladies back down the hill. The ladies were talking at a normal tone of voice between them, and the bear could hear this as easily as I could. He didn't care one bit as they rode along the road maybe 100 yards away. He just continued to feed on the berries, as the countdown to winter wasn't getting any longer.

I decided to try to use my predator call to get the bear interested in me. I popped it in my mouth and let loose a couple of very quiet whines. The bear basically melted into the dirt—meaning all movement of the bear stopped. I cannot explain how the bear got away without moving a leaf or making any sort of noise, but it did. This was not the first time I have witnessed such disappearing acts from bears, but when they do this, it never ceases to amaze me. I watched down into the ravine—again, nothing.

Well, that's hunting, I thought to myself. I turned around after sitting there waiting for a few minutes and made my way back up to the log landing. Now, from the landing, if I went straight on back to the main logging road that I came in on (the one the horses were on), there was a hillside that sprouted up, which had been logged a few years back and had stumps and brush with berries all over it. To my absolute surprise, there on the crest of the hill stood a bear on a tree stump. The bear was quiet with its broad protruding chest and thick legs resting on the log. I wish I could have gotten a good picture of him. He was completely silhouetted and was moving his head left to right looking all over for where that sound was coming from. He was obviously puzzled and interested. Of course, so was I!

Well, that's hunting! I thought to myself! Stunned at the turn of events, I was now looking at a bear who was clearly interested in what I was offering. I quickly tried to close some distance in the brush so I could clearly see the hillside the bear would come down on. With my open-sight .30-.30, I wasn't about to take a long shot. Currently, the bear was probably 300 yards out. I was hoping to call the bear to just below the middle of the hill, as there was a slight ledge there. If I could get it just past that spot, it would easily be in range. I watched him as he hopped down off the stump and worked his way downhill. I squealed a few times on the call, and now he was moving with a purpose toward me.

The plan was coming together; the bear was interested, on the move, and would soon be within my rifle range. I was still a little nervous about the earlier bear, which might have been behind me. It could easily come up out of the ravine and get right behind me. So, I tried to keep my eye out for that and coax this bear to me. Then it happened . . . random bear behavior.

On its way down the hill, the bear saw something better than the possibility of food (I used the screaming rabbit call); it saw actual food—a green huckleberry bush chock-full of red, luscious hucks! He turned on a dime, stopped right at that bush, and began tearing into it like the buffet it was. I called and called at the bear, who was just out of range. I changed pitch, tone, and so on, but the bear couldn't have cared less about my calling now. Its one-track mind was being fulfilled at that moment, and there was no reason to look any further. Well, that's hunting! I told myself. After some effort trying to coax the bear down off the hill, I eventually just sat and watched as the bear ate away, enjoying the moment.

It is not every day that you bear hunt and are fortunate enough to see two bears so close together, but that day I was blessed. I waited until dusk with no change in the bear's position, who still was eating away. The mosquitos had found me, and that made me pick up my pace back to the truck. After meeting up with my brother, he told me he had seen another bear up the hill but was unable to get a shot with his bow. All in all, it was a great night.

The bear that came out over the hill onto the stump was interesting. It was originally either right on the crest of the hill or even perhaps on the other side of it. It was interesting because that bear heard my calling from a distance even though I was using the call quietly. It was a testament to how well bears can hear (and that's true of predators in general), and it points out that we do not necessarily have to call them into our lap or have them commit to the call 100 percent. We just have to pique their interest enough to get a shot off. If I had my scoped rifle with me, I am sure I could have shot that bear but just as well. It would have been a nasty hill to get the bear off of anyway due to the brush.

TOO CLOSE FOR COMFORT!

This story is one that I will not soon forget. During the 2013 bear season, I decided to try something new for me. I wanted to use a mountain bike to help me to reach more hunting area. As you may have gathered, much of the hunting area that the public has access to in Washington is walk-in only or hunters can use bikes. There are some who use mountain bikes for hunting deer, elk, and bears. This was a new idea for me, and I thought it would be fun to try it. Of course, I had not ridden a bike since I was probably sixteen.

My mother-in-law Maryjane was kind enough to buy my wife and me bikes for Christmas a few years ago. They sat in our garage for a while, but they never left my thoughts for use in hunting. So, one day I picked mine up and took it out. While it took a little getting used to, I was excited to ride it. My legs were reminding me I hadn't done this in a while, and my rear end was wondering what the heck I was sitting on. Regardless of these qualms, on that mid-August, fairly warm, sunny day, I made my way up a hill. I had to go through a long straightaway, which had clear-cuts on it, but the hilltop, which I had never hunted before, was slightly overgrown with brush and butted up against a mature group of trees. I didn't happen to see a creek nearby, but the area certainly appeared to have potential for bears.

There were some open areas, some thick brushy areas, and the like. I had not called here before, so I was looking forward to it. I hopped off the bike and stashed it along the road out of sight from where I would be calling. I didn't want to give away my position or have something unnatural like a red bike sitting by me. I looked around for a defensive position, but the area I wanted to call down into didn't offer much defense. Therefore, I tucked myself along a small dirt embankment, and just above the embankment were trees about six to ten feet tall. A small dead-end road was right in front of me that opened up to a small dell with waist- to chest-high brush and various types of trees of varying heights.

I sat for a bit waiting for the normal noises to resume in the area before I interrupted them. I sat about ten minutes before I decided to start calling. In addition to having the embankment behind me, it was fairly dry out, so my hope was that I would hear something coming up behind me before it had the chance to pounce. As an added measure of defense, I placed my backpack behind me up high on my shoulders to help protect my neck in case of a cougar attack.

There was a light breeze from left to right. My rifle was across my lap pointing toward the very end of the road, which is where I anticipated something coming from. The crows were cawing and the squirrels were chattering—just another fine evening hunting and enjoying the outdoors. I wore a baseball cap with a mesh cover to help hide my face. My left hand was tucked under that mesh, so when I called, at least some of my movement would be concealed.

I began to call using a method I call eye lead. Instead of moving my head to look left and right, I slowly move my eyes all the way to the right or left, then I very slowly move my head an inch or two in that direction, then I use my eyes again to go all the way over, only moving my head when I have reached maximum range with my eyes. I want to be able to search the area while creating as little movement as possible. Remember, it is important to remain as still as possible when calling. If you are fidgeting with your hands or legs, that movement could easily give you away.

The sun was slightly behind me. This is important, as you don't want the sun flickering off your scope, wedding ring, and so forth. Try to use the glare of the sun to your advantage by forcing the bear to look into the sun, which makes you difficult to see. Midway through the set, about thirty minutes into it, I heard a squirrel start to give his warning. The squirrel sounded a little distant. This, again, is key. If a squirrel were going to warn about me calling, it would have done so fairly close and almost immediately. This squirrel was 100 yards away, or so, and began chattering after I had been making racket for a half hour. Something was likely on its way in.

Hearing a squirrel gives me a burst of energy, as I have the hope something is coming to the call. This was no different. My heart rate increased a bit, as did my calling. I smiled because I know how this game is played. I called for another five minutes or so and thought I heard a branch break . . . or did I? I wasn't sure, it could have been a tree popping like they do when they get warm. Sometimes they make a creaking sound when they get warm or cool as the wood expands or contracts.

I made the predator call sound as weak and helpless as I could, wanting it to sound desperate. Faint rustling sounds came from the brush in front of me—or was that the slight evening breeze? It wasn't the breeze—my sixth sense was tingling. It was one of those moments during which you think something is going to happen, but you are not sure. It was like being stuck on the edge of a cliff and waiting to fall—not sure if you will or not. It is intangible.

About forty-five minutes into the set, I was still crying away on the call. It is not uncommon for bears to take their sweet time in getting to you, so be sure to call for an hour, at least. Then I saw it—nothing but a flash of fur and its eyes locked onto me. It was within feet, all I could do was to swing my rifle to the left, in the direction of the oncoming animal, and my mind took a split second to process the situation. From directly across the road came a bobcat like a lightning bolt. My movement of swinging the gun was the only thing that stopped it from pouncing in my lap. The cat literally stopped right at the end of my barrel. I had a bobcat about three or four feet from me staring at me like lunch. I was dumbfounded.

I very slowly reached over to my side and turned on my little handheld camera. Nobody would believe this unless I got some footage. Amazingly, the cat did not bolt at my very slow movements but rather just slightly backed up. I was able to get a picture of the cat and some footage of it taking off. Holy cow, my adrenaline was flowing like a river! After I got my footage, the cat wagged its tail in disgust and bolted into the brush. Lucky for the cat, it was not bobcat season until September. It was likely for the best, as my .300 WSM would have split the thing in half had I fired.

After the cat ran for safety, my thoughts returned to the footage. Did I get it? I quickly checked the camera and, sure enough, I was able to get it! Wow, that was crazy, and to see how fast that bobcat was right on me was also insane. It very easily could have been a cougar. I have to say, having that bobcat almost hop into my lap was one of the coolest calling sessions I've had. After the bob left and I said some choice words fueled by adrenaline, I suppose, I ended the set and gathered up my equipment and thoughts. I did some calling in another clear-cut but with no luck, so

If having a bobcat almost bounce in your lap doesn't make you jump, I don't know what will!

I decided to return to the truck with the bike. I didn't get a bear that day, but, again, the experience was totally worth it on all levels! Not only did I get some cool footage and a great story, but I located a bobcat, which I could try to call or trap later in the season.

To recap, what I learned from this situation was pretty simple. Things happen very quickly when you are calling, so you must always be alert and ready. If that was a cougar or bear, it could have been a world of trouble for the both of us. I guess me and the cat, who probably has one fewer life now, got lucky on that day. Remember—be still, watch your wind, call with emotion, and good things will happen!

Calling predators, or bears specifically, is easy to start but hard to master. You really get to know a lot about bears when you try to call them. I trust these stories will provide you with what to expect when calling. Not all calling is fun and exciting. I have had plenty of boring call sessions when nothing showed up. At least, nothing I saw. In my opinion, other than baiting, calling for bears is the best way to hunt them. I hope you at least give calling bears a try; I think you will have the time of your life.

Chapter Seven

Field Dressing and Skinning

Here it is, the time when you have to bear down and the real work starts. You have studied areas, searched for the right spot, and were able to make a good shot on a bear; the hunting gods have smiled upon you. Now get to work, and don't let that bear go to waste!

There is no reason *not* to skin your own bear, especially if you have had any experience doing this to a deer, elk, or even smaller game. Practice makes perfect, and you will not learn unless you do it yourself. So take a good long look at this chapter before you head out bear hunting, and step into the woods with confidence on what to do after the shot! If you still require more info after reading this, the Internet is a great resource for learning. While reading from a book is great, with the Internet you can watch videos on any subject. Take a look at videos online for several how-to videos of skinning bears. The following are the exact steps I use to skin a bear for a rug or a full mount. I also go over how to skin a half mount and case skin, as well as cover field dressing. The following pictures are of my 2015 spring boar.

Before you start, make sure you have a sharp knife and a sharpener, as well as a bone saw. These are key. Bear hair seems to dull knives like you wouldn't believe. If you have a basic deer or elk skinning kit, that should suffice. Havalon knives make a wonderful product with disposable, razor-sharp blades. Make sure you have a sharpener, though, and use it! If you are having to use too much pressure, take a little break, sharpen that knife, and get back to it. A sharp knife saves a lot of energy and lessens the risk of an accidental slip. All right, let's get to it.

A game cart, with the help of some friends or family, is a great way to get a bear off the hill. That is, if the landscape allows. Pictured here are two of my brothers and my father. The bear in the cart is my younger brothers' three-legged bear.

1. The first thing you need to do is get the bear field dressed (gutted) as quickly as possible. Lay the bear on its back and spread the legs open. If you don't have any fellow hunters to help steady the animal, secure the bear as best you can using any rope, sash cord, or, my personal favorite, parachute cord. Tying the feet to trees or stumps can greatly ease the work needed to skin the bear properly. Also, it can help with safety, as you don't want to slip and cut or otherwise hurt yourself while skinning. I carry a pack of QuikClot in my backpack with gauze and other first-aid material just in case. You do not want to be out in the sticks and have a nasty, deep cut. Be prepared to do first aid on yourself.

    Do not cut the throat or make any unnecessary cuts to the hide. If you want a full body mount, *do not cut anything off the hide* (such as the penis). I repeat, do not cut anything at all off the hide. This will make it much easier for the taxidermist to properly sew up and represent your trophy. If you get a nick here or there in the hide, don't panic. We all do it, and usually the bear's hair is long enough that you will not even notice it. Plus, the taxidermist can sew up any noticeable cuts.

Note the single cut up the center of the bear.

2. Cut up the center of the bear using one straight cut from the anus to the mid-chest (cutting to one side around the genitalia). Be careful when you initially cut into the hide that you do not jab the knife edge into the body cavity. You want to ensure that you do not puncture the stomach or intestines, which will spoil

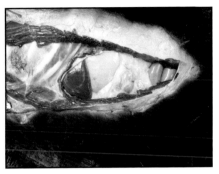

Notice the muscle and fat layer that is cut to expose the internal organs.

the meat. To properly cut through the hide, pierce the blade of the knife gently through the hide only. The next layer will be a fatty muscle layer. Cut through this layer gently a foot or so up toward the head.

The entrails should now be slightly pushing out of the hole you just made. This smaller incision allows you to see what you are cutting and allows your fingers to follow the underside of the knife as you cut. You should now be through the hide and the fatty muscle layer with the internal organs slightly exposed. Complete your incision all the way up the chest to a few inches up the breast plate. Do not cut all the way up to the neck, as it is not necessary.

3. We now need to expose and saw through the pelvis bone. You should be able to see where the muscles come together near the anus.

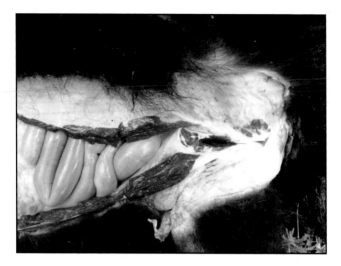

4. Cut through this muscle as shown. Use the bone saw and cut through the pelvis. It is going to take a bit of work to cut through. If the saw gets kind of clogged with muscle or bone matter, clean it off with your fingers.

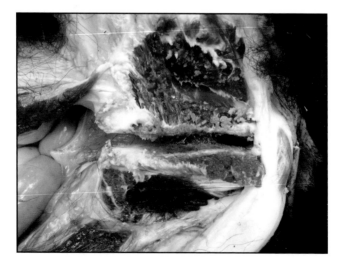

Be especially careful at this time, as the bladder is right in the way of your saw, as are the intestines. We do not want to puncture these items. Saw all the way through the bone so you can split the pelvis.

I want to touch on a product called the Havalon Hydra Double Bladed Hunting Knife. The system comes with seven styles of replaceable blades, three additional Baracuta blades, one each of fillet, hunter, and bone saw. In addition, there are twelve additional Piranta blades. Once I got this knife and bone saw combo, I decided to take my old standard bone saw, skinning knife, and larger skinner that were sheathed in leather out of my pack, as the Havalon Hydra was both lighter (with extra blades and saw) and sharper than my other knives. I am not the least disappointed with this decision. Staying true to my expectations of Havalon that I have already made by using their introduction knife for the last several years, I found the knife blades are all razor sharp, which helps immensely when skinning bears. The bone saw worked wonders on the other animals I took this season to allow for easy cutting and precision field dressing. If you, as a hunter or backpacker, are looking for a good-quality knife that is lightweight to bring along in the pack, I promise you this much, Havalon has got you covered. The different replacement blades, as well as the various sizes that come with the pack, can handle any big game you are ready to tackle. The Havalon Hydra Double Blade has you covered twice with the bone saw already attached to the knife—it truly expands and improves upon this otherwise stellar product.

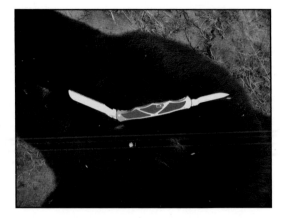

5. Now that the pelvis is split, take your smaller cutting knife and insert your arm into the body cavity. With the blade facing toward the rib cage, work the perimeter of the body cavity with the blade edge and try to go all the way around the ribcage. You are basically cutting the diaphragm and muscles that hold the internal organs in place. Make sure you cut all the way around the inside of the body cavity.

6. Reach up high into the cavity and find the esophagus with your hands. It will feel like a ribbed tube about two inches around. Cut the esophagus free. You may have to find the heart and cut it a bit loose, as well. Don't worry if you have to make a cut here or there inside to break everything loose. You should now be able to roll most of the organs out of the bear.

7. If at all possible, point the anus of the bear downhill, which will allow the organs to slip out easier. Gently work the organs out toward the anus and pay special attention not to rupture the intestines and the bladder.

8. Work the urinary tract gently through the cut you made, splitting the pelvis.

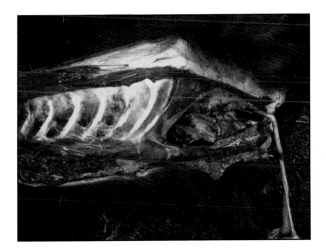

9. Roll the guts out; you should have a fairly intact gut pile.

10. The only thing left attached to the bear should be the urinary tract. Cut that long tube off as close to the body as you can, trying to ensure no urine spills on the meat.

11. You can rinse out the body cavity with some water if it is particularly dirty. Stay hydrated yourself or grab a snack if you're hungry. This will help you out. Remember, pee clear, pee often. Drink water!

12. Next, lay the front paws so that the pads of the foot are facing up toward you. (For example, if you were going to lay your hands down on a table with palms up.) Cut from the very center of the bottom of each paw pad (do not cut into the pad itself but just below the pad, at the hair line), down the front leg, center of the knee, and meet up to the first cut that you made at the center of the body of the bear, so the cut now connects in the center of the chest. Try to have the cuts leading from the pads, down the front legs, to the chest, line up with one another; this will make it easier for your taxidermist to do the necessary work. Take the back paws and do the same thing by cutting from the bottom of the foot pad hairline to the center of the body, where you started your cut near the anus. Again, try to have the cuts meet up. The more straight cuts you put on the hide, the better the final product will look.

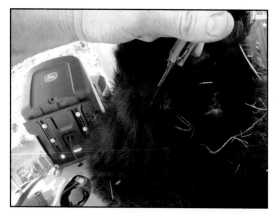

Line up your knife as shown here. Notice the knife will start the incision at the bottom center of the foot pad.

Begin loosening the hide from the body by cutting along the hide, but leave as much fat and meat on the body as possible. As you pull back the hide and cut it away from the body, you will soon notice where the hide is and where the fat begins. As you peel back the hide, if you begin to notice hair follicles right where you are cutting, you need to cut a little less close to the hide. It's better to have a bit of fat on the hide than to cut too close to the hairline. Next you will want to get the hide off and away from the legs. Once you get the wrists and ankles exposed, you can either saw through them or pop them off using your knife by cutting the ligaments in the joints. If you cut the right ligaments, you shouldn't have to saw much, if at all.

You should be able to feel where the feet bend at the joint by moving them back and forth with your hand. Expose and cut the ligaments to free up the feet.

The exposed joint before the ligaments are cut.

Ligament is beginning to be cut in this picture.

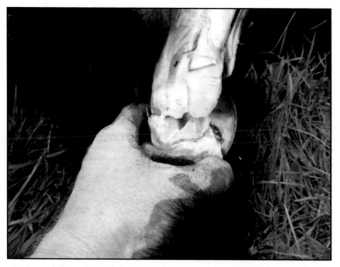

A view of the ankle of the bear.

Or, if you would like to try it, you can peel back the fur and skin close to the bones on all of the feet, then cut the feet and front paws free from the body (but leave them still attached to the hide). If you are not experienced in this or if you want to ensure a proper job, just leave the bones of the feet inside the hide. The taxidermist will do this for you, though there may be a cost involved depending on the taxidermist.

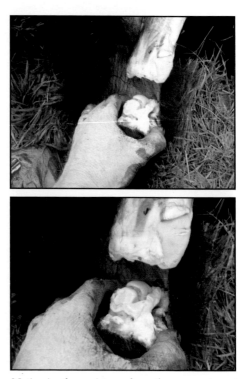

Notice in these pictures how the paw was not sawed through but just the ligaments were cut. This is an easy way to do it.

All claws should remain attached to the fur. I would suggest if this is your first time skinning a bear that you just cut the feet off as suggested. Again, leave the paws all attached to the fur, not the body. If you have skinned the feet, dispose of the bones from where you are working on the bear so you don't slip on them.

This is about how your bear should currently look.

This is how the bear should look once both front feet have been removed.

13. Leave the paws attached to the hide and separate the feet from the skinned body. Let them lay where they are at the moment. Then you can cut the tailbone and begin to drape the skin over the back of the head. If you prefer not to cut off the tailbone, cut the hide (with the bear still on its back) in the center of the tail all the way to the tip of the tail. Make sure to get all the way to the tip of the tail and *do not* leave a pocket of hide; go all the way to the very end of the bone on the tail. Bacteria can get into the little pocket of hide if the tail is not split properly and cause hair slippage. You can either split the tail down the center (the bottom part of the tail where partial bare skin is, not the top furry part) and take the bone out or leave it in for the taxidermist.

This is a view of the tail that is properly split down the center. Remember—do not leave any pocket on the tip of the tail skin.

14. You can repeat the process on the back legs, as you did to the front legs. They are shaped slightly differently, but the technique is basically the same. You will need to start to work the hide back from the back paws by exposing the ankle.

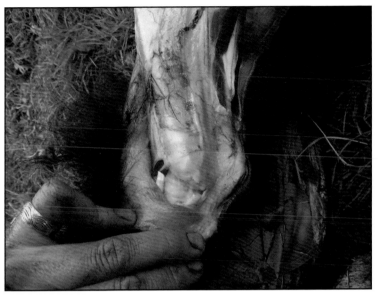

This is basically where a bears Achilles' heel would be, where the back heel meets the leg muscles. Peel back the hide and expose the ankle.

15. Expose the back heel area at the joint.

16. Cut the joint free from the foot as shown by cutting the ligaments and giving the foot a twist.

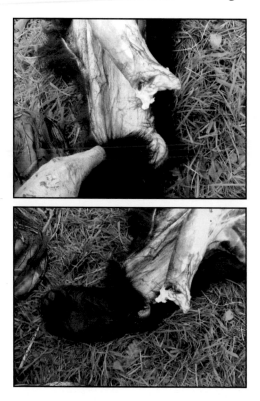

17. With the back foot free, you should be able to start to peel back the hide further.

Work the hide back with your knife to leave as much fat on the body as possible.

18. If at all possible, hang the bear by its back feet from a tree, barn timber, or other way to get it high up so you can stand and work.

Not the best way of doing it, but it worked!

Gravity will also help keep the hide sliding down the animal. If for whatever reason, you are not going to keep the hide, you can poke holes in the hide and place a finger or two in the hole to pull down on the hide with one hand as you cut it away from the body with another to help get it down faster. Skin the bear all the way to the base of the neck and saw the head off with your bone saw.

The hide is almost down to the head, where you can then separate the head from the body.

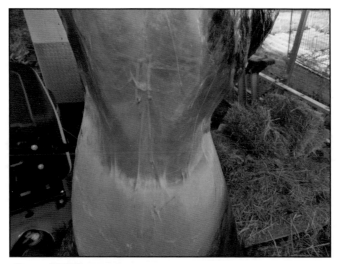

Almost down far enough.

Again, you can pop the vertebrae by finding a space between two vertebrae and cutting between them. You will get spinal fluid (a clear, slippery liquid) coming out of the spine once you separate the head. If you feel comfortable with it, you can skin the face, however I would *strongly* suggest that you leave the skull and hide attached and have your taxidermist do this if you are unfamiliar with the procedure.

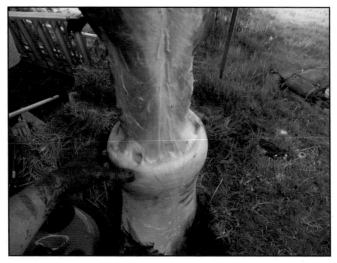

The hide is now down far enough to separate the skull.

Cutting through the esophagus before separating the skull.

Cut through the thick neck muscles so you can get access to the vertebrae.

Getting the nose and eyelids done correctly takes some skill and know-how. If this is your first time, leave it attached and ask to watch your taxidermist do it. If you want to try it, here is how:

As you roll the hide over the head, place your hand under the hide and find one ear. Place your thumb inside the ear. Continue to skin the hide with your free hand while using the ear hand to pull back the hide as you go. You will find a bump under the hide as you skin on either side of the head. This is the ear. Slowly pull back the hide and work the very bottom of the bump, cutting it close to the skull. As you cut into the bump base close to the skull, you shouldn't see any hair being cut, but you will be exposing the ear canal. Be careful not to cut your ear hand under the hide. Continue to pull back on the hide and cut free from the head until the ear is off the skull but still attached to the hide. Now go to the other side of the skull and repeat.

Now that the ears are free, continue to work the hide back slowly and free it from the skull. You will come to the eyes next. For this, make sure you have a sharp, delicate blade . . . again, Havalon knives are excellent for this type of work. (And, no, I am not sponsored by them.) Again, you are going to want one hand under the hide (basically place your thumb into the eye a bit) to help pull back the hide. Very gently and slowly, work the hide back and cut very close to the skull. You should very shortly see the eye socket. Remember to cut close to the skull, gently, as you are very close to the eyelids, and they are very delicate. As you start to see the eye socket, cut the hide close to the eye socket, kind of around the socket itself. This way, you free up the lid and lashes. You should be left with nothing but an exposed eyeball in the socket; the lid and lashes should be attached to the hide. Now do the same for the other side of the skull. Take your time.

Now that both ears and eyes are done, we have the nose and mouth to take care of. Pull the hide back and gently work the hide away from the skull, until you reach the back corners of the mouth. Again, you must take your time and gently work as close as you can to the skull and jawbone. As you pull the hide back, and cut the very back of the mouth, you will start to expose the jaws and teeth. Try to work both the left and right side of the mouth evenly. You essentially will be cutting down the jaw right where the underside of the lips connect to the gum line. As you continue to work your way down, you will have worked all the way to the nose. Use your delicate, sharp knife for this area, as well, and pull back the hide, but try to cut the cartilage away from the hide. This will expose the sinus cavity of the bear skull, and you should now be able to completely free the lips from the jaw. You should have the exposed bear skull ready to be European mounted if you so desire. Really take your time with doing all of this, so you do not cut off an eyelid or cut through the nose poorly. Patience and sharp knives, as well as technique, are really important for this process.

19. As you skinned, hopefully you tried to take the fat off the hide to leave just the hide. You should now have a hide with a head and four paws still attached (unless you skinned them out), as well as the tail and a skinned body. The same process can be followed if you want a full-body mount for the bear, but it is absolutely critical that you leave all parts on the body, including the anus. Do not cut any body parts off the hide if you want a full mount.

This is what you should be left with depending on if you left the skull and feet inside the hide or skinned them out.

20. If you want a half or shoulder mount, you can use the same method as above, or you can skin the bear back by the rear hips by cutting all the way around the body and then working your way to the head and front feet. As the taxidermist will not need the back legs to make a half mount, there is no reason to save that part of the hide unless you want to. The key to skinning for a half or shoulder mount is to ensure that you have left enough hide so the taxidermist can wrap the hide around the bear form. Remember, it's better to leave a little extra hide than not enough. I would cut just in front of the rear hips of the bear. This will ensure plenty of hide for the taxidermist to work with.

21. Do not forget to pull a tooth from the skull. Most states require you to turn in the tooth for aging purposes. On the upper jaw, it is the tooth directly behind the large canine. Your state game regulations will generally highlight this. An easy way to remove the tooth is to pry the tooth out gently with a small flathead screwdriver. Use a knife and cut the gum line from around the tooth to remove any tissue that holds the tooth. If you have to wait a little while before you can pull the tooth, put a stick vertically in the mouth so it does not seize shut when *rigor mortis* sets in. If it does seize shut, don't worry. You can cut away enough jaw muscle once the face is skinned to work the tooth out, generally speaking.

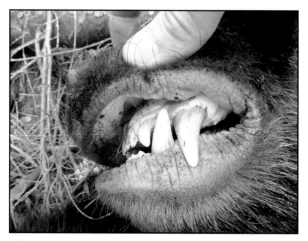

The tooth you want to pull is the little guy directly behind the upper or lower canine tooth.

22. Once the hide is off the bear, if it is going to be a few days (or, depending on the outside temperature, even a day) before you can get it to the taxidermist, fold the hide (fur to fur, so the meaty skin is facing out) and put it in the freezer. You want to keep it as cool and dry as possible. Water breeds bacteria. The hotter it is outside, the sooner you have to get the hide as cool as possible. Do not leave it in a plastic bag in the back of your truck for a few days, or you will be disappointed, as it will quickly rot. Do not roll the head up into a ball with the hide if you did not skin off the head; rather, leave the head on the outside of the folds. If it is folded in with the hide, it can take some time to freeze and some time to thaw, which increases the chance for hair slippage. It makes it easier on the taxidermist if it is not all balled up, as well. When folding the hide, fold the fur sides together so the skin side is exposed.

There is another option to skinning a bear that creates a unique hide display. I am a trapper here in Washington mainly for fun. I do not hit the trapping line too hard, but I do it more as a hobby and to get outside and enjoy the wildlife in the winter. You can case skin a black bear the same as most animals, except beavers, are prepared for trapping. It is a fairly simple procedure:

1. You have only one cut through the hide to make starting at the back legs. Cut from the bottom of the center of the pads just at the hairline, down the leg, and follow the cut to the anus. Do this on both legs.
2. Now, you have to peel the hide back and work on cutting it back away from the body of the bear by skinning the back feet first. Again, sharp knives are key, as you will soon learn if you haven't already. An extra person doesn't hurt here either but is not necessary.
3. If at all possible, hang the bear by its peeled back legs first. This allows gravity to keep things in place and pull the hide down for you.
4. Peel the hide down to the head and follow the same instructions I gave for skinning the head on the previous pages or save it for your taxidermist to do. Once you are all done peeling the bear and it is tanned, the hide should hang on a wall from its nose on display. Hang that bad boy on the wall in your house, and enjoy one of nature's greatest symbols.

Now that the bear is all skinned, you can work on deboning the meat. You will want to place the meat in breathable meat sacks—not plastic garbage bags. They make any number of styles of game bags. The best that I have found and enjoy using, not just for their quality but also their ability to be reused, is a brand called Caribou Game Bags. They can be washed over and over. Don't use a plastic garbage bag for a few reasons. First, lots of garbage bags are made from recycled plastic. You don't want that touching your game meat. Second, garbage bags do not breathe, and they trap in heat. With game meat, heat is the enemy, but if you're a hunter already, you know this. We want cool, clean game meat.

Another consideration is getting the loose fur off the meat. It doesn't matter how much you try not to, you are going to get some hair on the meat. Hair is dirty with bacteria and so on. It's not something you want on your upcoming meal. But if you try to sit there and pick it off, it takes forever. I have been told by some hunters that they use little blow torches to scorch the hair right off. Initially I thought this was a great way to do it until I spoke to a butcher friend of mine. His explanation makes complete sense. Burning the hair off not only melts the bacteria-filled fur onto the meat, but it also adds heat, both of which should be avoided. So, his solution is to take a Brillo pad (steel wool) and brush off the meat vigorously. This works like an absolute charm. Save the torch for making victory s'mores! Just grab that Brillo pad and swipe in one motion down and away from the meat. You will have hair-free meat in no time.

It doesn't matter if you are butchering the meat by yourself or if you are taking it somewhere to be deboned, the less hair, the better. Take your time to clean the meat as you put it in the bags. If you have the bear hanging, run the steel wool down the carcass to brush off the debris and hair before you start to take the meat off the bones. If it is cool enough out and you are going to let the bear hang overnight, cover the bear in a game bag (one that covers the whole body). Don't cover it in a plastic tarp. Again, you want the meat to breathe, to keep bugs off it, and to keep it as dry as possible. Leave the fat on the bear until you are ready to process it to help protect the meat from drying out too much. Try to seal the bags with duct tape to keep the flies and hornets away, or simply tie them to secure them.

Remove bear meat the same way you would a deer or an elk. A word of caution: if it's a bit warm out, maybe after a summer bear hunt, you have to let the bear hang overnight. If you have already boned out the hams, slice the large hams down the middle, as well as the large neck muscles to open them up a bit. This helps cool the center of the meat, which can stay warm for some time after the animal is dead and even turn bad on you if left too long. The same should be exercised for large bull elk.

I have found when deboning a game animal, it is best to try and separate the meat into certain sacks that way you know what you have and where it is. I usually put stew meat, rib meat, or what will be used as burger into one group of sacks. Roasts might go into a couple of sacks to help separate the weight. Shoulders and leg meat into another. Back straps and tenderloins usually go together.

A side note: If it is the middle of the summer with raging heat and you are going bear hunting, try to limit your hunting to an area where you can quickly get the meat and hide out so it can cool. Bear meat spoils quickly in the heat, so the sooner you can prepare it, the better. You don't want to lose your meat or have hair slippage because you downed a bear ten miles back and it takes you two days to get it all out. Just my two cents, there.

The same principle applies when deboning as when you were skinning: sharpen your knives often. Try to avoid hitting the bones, as this dulls your knife faster. Don't forget to get the meat between the ribs if you are not taking the rib cage itself. You would be surprised how much meat there is between the ribs—good burger meat. Also, locate the tenderloins inside the body cavity, close to the rear and under the back.

Another method some people use is called a gutless method, where they do not bother gutting the animal. This might work on deer or elk, animals from which you do not want the hide, but most people I know want to retain the bear hide. There are some out there who already have enough hides and just want the meat—but I love bear hides!

The gutless method is fairly easy. Lay the bear on its back. Do your center cut up from the anus to the chest, all the way up to the neck. Roll the bear on its side and make cuts from the center of the paws down the legs and to the center cut. Now, start to peel back the hide, pulling it back as you go. Disconnect the feet from the body. If you get to where you have half of the bear skinned, you can start to debone the bear and place the meat in the sacks. Debone the whole side of the bear that has been skinned and is facing up. Do not bother gutting it. Once this is done, roll the body on the other side and repeat.

You should be left with nothing but a bear skeleton and a large intact gut. Take note, I know states such as Alaska are very specific about wasting any game meat, and they might easily consider this wasting, as the tenderloins are left inside. The point is to check your regulations and make sure you harvest as much of the animal as possible. The animal deserves it and, as hunters, we should require it. Honor that animal by using as much of it as possible.

Another interesting feature about bears is that their penis, or baculum, is bone. There are some people who will take this out of the boar and clean it to use for a drink swizzle stick or other decorative purpose. I usually just use my finger to stir my drinks, but to each his or her own. If you want a swizzle stick, I know where you can find one.

To recap, bear meat is similar to elk, deer, or any other big game you are eating. You want to keep it as cool and dry as possible. And you want to have it cooled as quickly as possible. Following simple rules of using breathable game bags, extracting the animal quickly from the hunting grounds so you can prepare the hide and meat, and keeping it clean and dry are simple and basic rules to follow. Abide by these rules, and you are sure to have a wonderful hide and plenty of great meals to enjoy with friends and family.

Chapter Eight

From Field to Kitchen

So, your bear hunt was successful. You have field dressed the bear properly, hauled it out of the woods, and hopefully sent the hide off to the taxidermist for a wonderful mount or rug to be enjoyed in your home for years to come. Let's not forget why we hunt in the first place—the wonderful game meat. The following are some of my family's favorite dishes featuring bear. Whether you have the bear butchered or do it yourself, remember to get as much of the fat off the animal before processing or cooking it into a final meal.

Bear fat is not marbled into the muscles like, say, beef. It is layered above the meat for the most part. Cut away as much of this greasy fat and silver skin as possible. It doesn't taste all that pleasant. If you are going to grind some bear into burger, which is a great use of the meat, do not forget to add some pig fat to the mix—around 20 percent depending on your taste. This will help keep the meat together when you make it into patties and add a bit of flavor. If you do not want to add fat to the meat because you like the taste and the healthy aspects of a low-fat meat, you can use egg and olive oil to help bind the burger together before cooking.

Bear fat can be used to help waterproof your boots (although they will smell like a bear). I have done this before, and it works great. Just heat up the boots with a hair dryer and apply the fat liberally throughout the boots. Pay special attention to the seams. Heat the fat with the dryer to ensure it soaks into the leather.

Finally, there is the trichinosis issue and *Toxoplasma gondii*, the parasites that cause the diseases trichinosis and toxoplasmosis in humans.

This is a species of roundworm that is common in bears and has been found in pigs but has since been eradicated in mass-produced meat. You can get trich by eating the undercooked meat of an infected animal, which contains the larvae of the worm. It's a nasty little ailment, and you can avoid it by fully cooking the meat, like you would pork, or by freezing the meat at subzero temperatures for more than thirty days. Either way you choose to do it, don't go eating any bear sushi. If you start to show symptoms of trich after eating bear, seek medical attention and let them know what you have eaten recently. Symptoms include diarrhea, abdominal discomfort, nausea, fever, fatigue, and vomiting. I am not writing this to turn you off from black-bear meat, as it really takes to spices wonderfully and is a delicacy, but I wanted to inform you of the possibility of being exposed to the parasite. Proper cooking techniques will ensure that your bear meat is safe to eat.

Just like your favorite pork product, the proper cooking time for bear meat is about 375 degrees Fahrenheit for twenty to twenty-five minutes per pound. Use a meat thermometer to ensure that the internal cooking temperature reaches 160 degrees for three minutes or more before eating. Cook until there is no pink meat or juice coming from the meat, especially around the bones. Bear meat really makes some wonderful summer sausage and pepperoni sticks if you have the time to make them. Now, let's move on to some good bear recipes.

This chili dish is a family favorite around my household and, more importantly, it is quick and easy. Nothing says comfort food like a hot bowl of chili on a cold afternoon or evening with a side of buttery cornbread and honey.

Brown Sugar Bear Chili

Prep time fifteen minutes, cook time two to six hours depending on how long you want it to simmer. Serves six to eight.

    1 pound ground bear meat
    1 large onion, chopped
    3 to 4 spoons of minced garlic (or 3 to 4 cloves, minced)
    1 can (14 1/2 ounces) diced tomatoes
    1 fresh tomato, chopped
    1 can black beans
    1 can red beans

Photography and styling by Adrian Perry.

1 can (16 ounces) baked beans, drained
3 tablespoons salsa
6 tablespoon brown sugar
5 tablespoon chili powder
1/2 teaspoon garlic salt (or onion salt)
1/2 teaspoon pepper
3/4 cup hot water
1 bowl grated cheddar cheese

Directions: Brown ground meat in a skillet. Drain fat if needed. Combine all ingredients in a large Crock-Pot. Cover and simmer on high for two hours, stirring occasionally. If you want to simmer it longer, drop the temperature down to low and let simmer for another four hours or so. The longer it simmers . . . the better it tastes. Serve with cornbread, if you wish. While the ingredient proportions, specifically the brown sugar and chili powder, are what I start with when I begin to cook the chili, I often taste the chili throughout the cooking process and add more brown sugar and chili powder to the mix depending on taste. By doing so, you can ensure that you have the spiciness and sweetness to your liking. I personally do not like super-spicy foods, so I usually end up with a sweeter chili with a decent kick of spice to it. Depending on how well your Crock-Pot seals, you may want to add a cup of water to the mixture throughout the cooking process to make the chili soupier. Leftovers of this chili are great, but I can't promise that you will have any!

Photography and styling by Adrian Perry.

This next dish is a version of something I grew up on. Simple, hearty, and ready to go in no time.

The Hungry Hunter's Casserole

Prep time, fifteen minutes, cook time an hour to an hour and a half depending on oven. Serves about four hungry hunters!

Ingredients:

   1 pound ground bear burger (or any other burger)
   1 can of corn, drained
   1 can of green beans, drained
   4 to 6 red potatoes (medium size)
   Grated cheddar cheese (a soup bowl full)
   2 cans cream of mushroom soup

Photography and styling by Adrian Perry.

Directions:
1. Brown bear burger in pan, drain as needed.
2. Put burger in bottom of casserole pan (medium size).
3. Pour cream of mushroom soup over burger and spread evenly with a spatula.
4. Pour drained corn and green beans over burger evenly.
5. Clean and slice potatoes into chips or thin slices.
6. Lay potatoes (uncooked) flat over the top of burger/soup mix.
7. Preheat oven to 350 degrees. Cover casserole dish in tin foil
8. Cook for an hour to hour and a half, or until potatoes are tender to a fork.
9. Ten minutes before removing, sprinkle shredded cheese over the dish. Leave tin foil off casserole to melt and brown cheese. Let stand five minutes before serving.

Enjoy!

Photography and styling by Adrian Perry.

Bear Stroganoff

Who doesn't like meat, noodles, and sour cream? Maybe your heart doctor. Prep time ten minutes, cook time twenty minutes. Serves four.

Photography and styling by Adrian Perry.

Ingredients:

1 pound bear burger or bear meat cut into thin two-inch strips

24-ounce container of sour cream

1 onion half, finely chopped

1 cup mushrooms, chopped

1 half package of egg noodles

Salt and pepper to taste

1 Tbsp of olive oil

Directions:

1. Cook the bear burger or cut strips on medium heat in a large frying pan using a tablespoon of olive oil. Brown meat with finely chopped onion and mushrooms. Add salt and pepper to taste.

2. While cooking the meat, bring water to a boil in pot and follow the directions on the egg-noodle package. Cook noodles accordingly.

3. Drain noodles.

4. Add noodles to meat and stir. Transfer to a serving bowl. Add the sour cream and stir. *Note*: the sour cream is subjective—some people like lots of sour cream in the Stroganoff, while others prefer a dab of it. If this is the case, the sour cream can be left out and made available to the dinner guests so they can add the correct amount for their palate.

Bear Roast (in a Slow Cooker)

This is a quick, easy, no fuss dinner idea. Prep time ten minutes, cook time six to eight hours depending on temperature of the Crock-Pot. Serves four to five.

Photography and styling by Adrian Perry.

Ingredients:

1-3 pound bear roast, trimmed with no fat

1 (10 1/2 ounce) can cream of mushroom soup

1 (10 1/2 ounce) can hot water or 1 (10 1/2 ounce) can brewed coffee

1 (1 ounce) envelope dry onion soup mix

2 teaspoons of your favorite packaged steak seasoning (low sodium) McCormick brand has some good variations

3 carrots cut up into 2 to 3 inch sections

4 large red potatoes, quartered

Large onion, quartered

Directions:

1. Place roast in Crock-Pot. Surround roast with potatoes and carrots.
2. Using a large measuring cup, gradually mix hot water or coffee with cream of mushroom soup until smooth. Pour it over roast.
3. Sprinkle with onion soup mix and steak seasoning. Only use about half of the steak seasoning package or it becomes too salty, in my opinion.
4. Cook on high setting for six hours, then lower the temperature to the low setting until ready to serve.

Photography and styling by Adrian Perry.

Breakfast Bear Sausage Scramble with Biscuits

This next dish is wonderful for the working man or woman. Not only does it offer a good meal with little prep time, but it can be reheated the next day for a quick dish on the go. Prep time fifteen minutes, bake time thirty to thirty-five minutes. This is a crazy good way to start your day.

Photography and styling by Adrian Perry.

Ingredients:

1 pound ground bear sausage
12 to 14 eggs
1 tube of buttermilk biscuits (or cinnamon rolls)
1 cup grated cheddar cheese in bowl
Diced chives

Directions:

1. In a large pan, brown the bear sausage and drain if needed.
2. Scramble all eggs in a large mixing bowl.
3. Add the browned bear sausage and cheese to the egg mixture.
4. Use casserole pan (medium sized), spray with Pam or grease with butter.
5. Take one tube of biscuits (or cinnamon rolls) and layer the bottom of the pan.
6. Pour the bowl of eggs, cheese, and sausage over the biscuits.
7. Place diced chives on top of that mixture.
8. Bake at 350 degrees for 30 to 35 minutes.
9. Check center of pan to make sure the eggs have been cooked fully before serving.

Photography and styling by Adrian Perry.

Black Bear Back Strap Fajitas

Prep time ten minutes, cook time twenty minutes. Taco Tuesday? Back strap fajitas are one of my favorites. They are quick, easy, and the family loves them. Here is how I like to prepare them. Serves about four.

Photography and styling by Adrian Perry.

Thinly sliced meat with some salt and pepper for taste.

Ingredients:

 1 section of bear back strap, about the length of your palm, thinly sliced (deer or elk works, too)

 1 whole yellow onion, chopped

 Taco seasoning to taste

 Few dashes salt

 3 to 4 grindings of fresh peppercorns

 1½ cups salsa

 1 fresh tomato, chopped

 Half a head freshly cut lettuce, chopped

 Cheddar cheese (soup bowl full)

 Small amount of olive oil

 One lime, wedged

 One sweet red pepper, chopped

 Tortillas, corn or flour

Directions:

1. Take the back strap, wash, and cut it into thin strips of varied length. I like to put them in a container and marinate them with salsa for a few hours before I cook them. Douse with salt and pepper. Place in fridge.

2. Cut up a whole onion and set aside. Cut thick or thin to your liking. I prefer slightly thicker cuts for fajitas.

3. Cut up red pepper and set aside. Again, thick or thin—your choice.

4. Cut up lettuce and set aside.

5. Shred cheese and set aside.

6. In a medium frying pan, place a small amount of olive oil and turn on medium heat.

7. Place the thinly sliced back strap into the pan. Pour all of the salsa that the meat was marinating in into the pan. Cook uncovered on medium heat.

8. Add the diced onion. Stir frequently.

9. Add a couple of teaspoons of taco seasoning for flavor. Add salt and pepper.

10. Add the diced sweet red pepper once the meat is turned slightly brown.

11. Sauté the onions until they are soft and slightly brown. The meat will cook quickly, so only cook until all the meat is browned. Fully cook the bear meat, but do not overcook to avoid drying out the meat.

12. While cooking the meat, heat up a small frying pan to lightly toast the tortillas. Use your oven on low to keep them warm while you finish cooking the meat.

13. Serve with sour cream, salsa of your choice, lettuce, tomatoes, and shredded cheese (naturally). Best served while hot. Squeeze lime wedges over meat for flavor, if desired.

14. If you find that you have a bit too much water in the pan from the salsa, just turn the heat on high and cook uncovered for a few minutes to evaporate the water.

Photography and styling by Adrian Perry.

Blueberry Layered Dessert

Prep time fifteen minutes, ready to eat in several hours.

So, what is a good hunting dish without a good hunting dessert? After all, hunting camp isn't just about success, telling lies, and good friends. It's about the food! The next recipe is not from bear meat, obviously, but it does contain what the bears like to eat—mainly blueberries and, yes, a bit of sugar. Therefore, I decided to include it. The blueberry Jell-O dessert has been a family favorite since I was a boy. There is not a Thanksgiving or Christmas at my father's house where this dish is not devoured and relished by pretty much my whole family. I hope you enjoy it as much as I do. As I write this, Thanksgiving is just around the corner, and I am so excited to eat this tasty dish! Serves nine.

Photography and styling by Adrian Perry.

Ingredients:

    2 cups whipping cream (liquid)

    1 1/3 cup sugar

    2 (1 ounce) envelopes Knox gelatin

    1/2 cup cold water

    2 teaspoons vanilla extract

    2 pints sour cream

    1 (3 ounce) package strawberry Jell-O

1 cup boiling water

2 cups fresh or frozen blueberries, huckleberries, or sliced strawberries.

Directions:

1. Heat whipping cream and sugar together until scalding. Stir frequently while heating to avoid scorching.

2. Dissolve gelatin in cold water. Add dissolved gelatin mixture to hot mixture and stir well. Remove from heat.

3. Add vanilla and sour cream and blend well using a wire whip, if necessary. Pour into a circular spring-release pan that you would use for cheesecake or a 9″ × 13″ casserole dish.

4. Dissolve Jell-O in boiling water, add blueberries. Mix and cool. It is important to let the cream mixture cool and harden up before you pour the Jell-O mixture on top of it. Allow several hours for the cream mixture to cool in a fridge. Once the cream mixture is cooled and set, pour Jell-O mixture over cream, chill to set Jell-O for several hours or overnight in the fridge.

Photography and styling by Adrian Perry.

So, I hope after reading this chapter, you are either hungry, or you are full from eating all this bear goodness. I wanted to express how easy it is for you to make your own burger, which is a great use for the meat between a bear's ribs and any other scraps of quality meat you didn't have cut and wrapped. Any sporting goods store, or even Wal-Mart or other retailer, will sell a meat grinder, which is about all you need to make some low-fat quality burger for the family.

There is something satisfying about butchering your own game. Support your local butcher, but sometimes doing it your own way is the way it should be done.

The biggest concern when making your own burger, especially with bear meat because it is such a lean meat, is keeping the meat from falling apart when you cook it. Some people add pork fat to it—about 20 percent. I have also seen people add bacon to it by grinding it together with the bear meat. Egg is also added to burger to help hold it together. That is a trick my wife showed me. Pour a little olive oil in with it to add a bit of moisture. My point is, don't feel like you have to trust your meat with a butcher. If you do place trust in a butcher to take care of your meat, ask if you are getting your own meat back or just general meat of the same type. It is important to get your own meat back, as you do not know how the other person took care of their meat, not to mention the legalities of having game meat in your freezer that does not match, if a DNA match were to be done.

Bear meat is a wonderful addition to any big-game hunter's diet. Given half the chance, it can be enjoyed just like elk, deer, pheasant, grouse, and all the rest of nature's goodness. Just remember to fully cook bear, and feel free to substitute it for beef in any of your favorite dishes. You might be pleasantly surprised.

Epilogue

Writing, specifically writing about my outdoor experiences, including bear hunting, has been a passion of mine for the last few years. I greatly enjoy being able to share my adventures and express my love of the outdoors with anyone who is willing to listen or read about it. Writing this book has been a great pleasure, not only due to the satisfaction of completing my second book but also reliving, retelling, and truly trying to teach others how to become successful bear hunters.

Strategies for bear hunting can really be summed up quite simply—find a food source for that time of year with limited human interaction in the area, some water, and some good cover, and you will likely find bears.

Obviously, there are many finer points to the subject, which I hope I have thoroughly covered in this book. Just remember what you learned from the book and keep your eyes out for the signs of bear, such as stripped trees, scat, tracks, reports from other hunters or hikers, and food sources. Really hone your craft when it comes to shot placement—practice like it is real life. Learn as much as you can about black bears and you will find success, I am sure of it. Remember, hunting bears is not the easiest thing you will do, nor is it the most difficult. It is called hunting for a reason, so if you don't find success right away, just keep at it. You will only gain more knowledge and, statistically, the longer you are out looking for bear, the better the odds that you will find one!

As you take this knowledge and apply it in your bear hunting, please also pass it along to the younger generation. When I go to some benefit banquets, friends of National Rifle Association dinners, and the like, I often notice how old the crowd is. We need youth in our tradition, so be sure to pass it along to whomever takes an interest. To keep hunting (and trapping) alive, we have to get as many young people involved in these wonderful pastimes (really, a way of life) as possible.

In closing, I would like to thank a few people and companies. My beautiful wife, Amy, of course, for putting up with me going out hunting as often as I do. I guess since she said I can do so in our wedding vows (which I have framed for proof, by the way), there is little she can dispute on the subject. Regardless, thanks is in order. To FOXPRO, Havalon Knives, Montana Decoy, Wayne Carlton, and Dale Denny from Bearpaw Outfitters, thank you for your effort and overall support. I was really blown away by my interaction with all of you. These are truly fine companies and people whom I would encourage anyone reading this book to support.

Thanks to my lifelong friend, Justin Haug—many of the pictures taken in this book are your fine work. Your talent in photography greatly added to the value of this book, and many of my childhood and adult fond memories have you in them. Thanks for being you, my friend. (Go Cougs!) Fred Moyer, thanks for the great photos! Lastly, to Adrian Perry (www. adrianjosephine.com), your talent in food artistry and your eye for artistic presentation of dishes was amazing. Thanks for your efforts. You are my favorite vegetarian, which is saying quite a lot.

My 2015 spring bear with a long, glorious coat.